AN ENEMY OF THE PEOPLE

Henrik Ibsen was born in 1828 in Skien, Telemark, Norway. When he was eight years old his father's business became bankrupt, and the rest of his youth was spent in poverty. At fifteen he was apprenticed to an apothecary in Grimstad and began to prepare for medical school. He was thus required to learn Latin, an undertaking that led to his interest in the character of the Roman traitor Catiline. His first play, *Catiline*, published in 1850, was a failure; but in the same year he moved to Christiania, where a second play was performed with success. In 1851 he became stage manager of a theatre in Bergen, with a contract obliging him to write a new play every year. In 1857 he was appointed director of the Norwegian Theatre in Christiania, and in 1863 he won a scholarship for travel to Italy, where he wrote *Brand* and *Peer Gynt*. His standing in the theatre was now established, and in the years that followed he wrote first a group of social-problem plays (including *A Doll's House* and *An Enemy of the People*), then psychological dramas (among them, *The Wild Duck* and *Rosmersholm*), and finally the transcendent symbolist pieces (*The Master Builder, Little Eylof, John Gabriel Borkman,* and *When We Dead Awaken*). He died in Christiania in 1906.

Arthur Miller was born in New York City in 1915 and studied at the University of Michigan. His plays include *All My Sons* (1947), *Death of a Salesman* (1949), *The Crucible* (1953), *A View from the Bridge* and *A Memory of Two Mondays* (1955), *After the Fall* (1964), *Incident at Vichy* (1965), *The Price* (1968), *The Creation of the World and Other Business* (1972), and *The American Clock* (1980). He has also written two novels, *Focus* (1945) and *The Misfits*, which was filmed in 1960, and the text for *In Russia* (1969), *Chinese Encounters* (1979), and *In the Country* (1977), three books of photographs by Inge Morath. His most recent works include a memoir, *Timebends* (1987), and the plays *The Ride Down Mt. Morgan* (1991), *The Last Yankee* (1993), *Broken Glass* (1994), and *Mr. Peters' Connections* (1999), *Echoes Down the Corridor: Collected Essays, 1944–2000,* and *On Politics and the Art of Acting* (2001). He has twice won the New York Drama Critics Circle Award, and in 1949 he was awarded the Pulitzer Prize. He was the recipient of the National Book Foundation 2001 Medal for Distinguished Contribution to American Letters, he was awarded with the prize Prince of Asturias of Letters in 2002, and most recently in 2003 was awarded the Jerusalem Prize.

Arthur Miller's

adaptation of

AN ENEMY
OF THE PEOPLE

by Henrik Ibsen

PENGUIN BOOKS

PENGUIN BOOKS

Published by the Penguin Group

Penguin Group (USA) Inc., 375 Hudson Street, New York, New York 10014, U.S.A.

Penguin Group (Canada), 90 Eglinton Avenue East, Suite 700, Toronto,
Ontario, Canada M4P 2Y3 (a division of Pearson Penguin Canada Inc.)

Penguin Books Ltd, 80 Strand, London WC2R 0RL, England

Penguin Ireland, 25 St Stephen's Green, Dublin 2, Ireland (a division of Penguin Books Ltd)

Penguin Group (Australia), 250 Camberwell Road, Camberwell,
Victoria 3124, Australia (a division of Pearson Australia Group Pty Ltd)

Penguin Books India Pvt Ltd, 11 Community Centre, Panchsheel Park, New Delhi – 110 017, India

Penguin Group (NZ), cnr Airborne and Rosedale Roads,
Albany, Auckland 1310, New Zealand (a division of Pearson New Zealand Ltd)

Penguin Books (South Africa) (Pty) Ltd, 24 Sturdee Avenue,
Rosebank, Johannesburg 2196, South Africa

Penguin Books Ltd, Registered Offices: 80 Strand, London WC2R 0RL, England

First published in the United States of America by Viking Penguin Inc. 1951
Published in Penguin Books 1977

50   49   48   47   46   45   44   43   42   41

LIBRARY OF CONGRESS CATALOGING IN PUBLICATION DATA
Ibsen, Henrik, 1828–1906.
Arthur Miller's adaptation of An enemy of the people.
(Penguin plays)
Translation of En folkefiende. I. Miller, Arthur, 1915–
II. Title. III. Title: An enemy of the people.
PT8862.A37M5   1977   839.8'2'26   77-24276
ISBN 0 14 048.140 0

Printed in the United States of America
Set in Linotype Baskerville

Preface

1

At the outset it ought to be said that the word "adaptation" is very distasteful to me. It seems to mean that one writer has ventured into another's chickencoop, or worse, into the sacred chamber of another's personal creations and rearranged things without permission. Most of the time an adaptation is a playwright's excuse for not writing his own plays, and since I am not yet with my back against that particular wall, I think it wise to set down what I have tried to do with *An Enemy of the People,* and why I did it.

There is one quality in Ibsen that no serious writer can afford to overlook. It lies at the very center of his force, and I found in it—as I hope others will—a profound source of strength. It is his insistence, his utter conviction, that he is going to say what he has to say, and that the audience, by God, is going to listen. It is the very same quality that makes a star actor, a great public speaker, and a lunatic. Every Ibsen play begins with the unwritten words: "Now listen here!" And these words have shown me a path through the wall of "entertainment," a path that leads beyond the formulas and dried-up precepts, the pretense and fraud, of the business of the stage. Whatever else Ibsen has to teach, this is his first and greatest contribution.

In recent years Ibsen has fallen into a kind of respectful obscurity that is not only undeserved but really quite disrespectful of culture—and a disservice to the theater besides. I decided to work on *An Enemy of the People* because I had a private wish to demonstrate that Ibsen is really pertinent today, that he is not "old-fashioned," and, implicitly, that those who condemn him are themselves misleading our theater and our playwrights into a blind alley of senseless sensibility, triviality, and the inevitable waste of our dramatic talents; for it has become the fashion for plays to reduce the "thickness" of life to a fragile facsimile, to avoid portraying the complexities of life, the contradictions of character, the fascinating interplay of cause and effect that have long been part of the novel. And I wished also to buttress the idea that the dramatic writer has, and must again demonstrate, the right to entertain with his brains as well as his heart. It is necessary that the public understand again that the stage is *the* place for ideas, for philosophies, for the most intense discussion of man's fate. One of the masters of such a discussion is Henrik Ibsen, and I have presumed to point this out once again.

2

I have attempted to make *An Enemy of the People* as alive to Americans as it undoubtedly was to Norwegians, while keeping it intact. I had no interest in exhuming anything, in asking people to sit respectfully before the work of a celebrated but neglected writer. There are museums for such activities; the theater has no truck with them, and ought not to have.

And I believed this play could be alive for us because its central theme is, in my opinion, the central theme of our social life today. Simply, it is the question of whether the democratic guarantees protecting political minorities ought to be set aside in time of crisis. More personally, it is the question of whether one's vision of the truth ought to be a source of guilt at a time when the mass of men condemn it as a dangerous and devilish lie. It is an enduring theme—in fact, possibly the most endur

Preface

ing of all Ibsen's themes—because there never was, nor will there ever be, an organized society able to countenance calmly the individual who insists that he is right while the vast majority is absolutely wrong.

The play is the story of a scientist who discovers an evil and, innocently believing that he has done a service to humanity, expects that he will at least be thanked. However, the town has a vested interest in the perpetuation of that evil, and his "truth," when confronted with that interest, must be made to conform. The scientist cannot change the truth for any reason disconnected with the evil. He clings to the truth and suffers the social consequences. At rock bottom, then, the play is concerned with the inviolability of objective truth. Or, put more dynamically, that those who attempt to warp the truth for ulterior purposes must inevitably become warped and corrupted themselves. This theme is valid today, just as it will always be, but some of the examples given by Ibsen to prove it may no longer be.

I am told that Ibsen wrote this play as a result of his being practically stoned off the stage for daring to present *Ghosts*. The plot is supposed to have come from a news item which told of an Hungarian scientist who had discovered poisoned water in the town's water supply and had been pilloried for his discovery. If this was the case, my interpretation of the theme is doubly justified, for it then seems beyond doubt that Ibsen meant above and beyond all else to defend his right to stand "at the outpost of society," alone with the truth, and to speak from there to his fellow men.

However, there are a few speeches, and one scene in particular, which have been taken to mean that Ibsen was a fascist. In the original meeting scene in which Dr. Stockmann sets forth his—and Ibsen's—point of view most completely and angrily, Dr. Stockmann makes a speech in which he turns to biology to prove that there are indeed certain individuals "bred" to a superior apprehension of truths and who have the natural right to lead, if not to govern, the mass.

If the entire play is to be understood as the working-out of this speech, then one has no justification for contending that it is other than rascist and fascist—certainly it could not be thought of as a defense of any democratic idea. But, structurally speaking, the theme is not wholly contained in the meeting scene alone. In fact, this speech is in some important respects in contradiction to the actual dramatic working-out of the play. But that Ibsen never really believed that idea in the first place is amply proved by a speech he delivered to a workers' club after the production of *An Enemy of the People*. He said then: "Of course I do not mean the aristocracy of birth, or of the purse, or even the aristocracy of the intellect. I mean the aristocracy of character, of will, of mind—that alone can free us."

I have taken as justification for removing those examples which no longer prove the theme—examples I believe Ibsen would have removed were he alive today—the line in the original manuscript that reads: "There is no established truth that can remain true for more than seventeen, eighteen, at most twenty years." In light of genocide, the holocaust that has swept our world on the wings of the black ideology of racism, it is inconceivable that Ibsen would insist today that certain individuals are by breeding, or race, or "innate" qualities superior to others or possessed of the right to dictate to others. The man who wrote *A Doll's House*, the clarion call for the equality of women, cannot be equated with a fascist. The whole cast of his thinking was such that he could not have lived a day under an authoritarian regime of any kind. He was an individualist sometimes to the point of anarchism, and in such a man there is too explosive a need for self-expression to permit him to conform to any rigid ideology. It is impossible, therefore, to set him beside Hitler.

3

On reading the standard translations of Ibsen's work it quickly became obvious that the false impressions that have been connected with the man would seem to be justified were he to be produced in "translated" form. For one thing, his language in English sounds impossibly pedantic. Combine this with the fact that he wore a beard and half-lenses in his eyeglasses, and that his plays have always been set forth with yards of fringe on every tablecloth and drapery, and it was guaranteed that a new production on the traditional basis would truly bury the man for good.

I set out to transform his language into contemporary English. Working from a pidgin-English, word-for-word rendering of the Norwegian, done by Mr. Lars Nordenson, I was able to gather the meaning of each speech and scene without the obstruction of any kind of English construction.

For instance, Mr. Nordenson, working from the original Norwegian manuscript, set before me speeches such as: "But, dear Thomas, what have you then done to him again?" Or: "The Mayor being your brother, I would not wish to touch it, but you are as convinced as I am that truth goes ahead of all other considerations." Or: "Well, what do you say, Doctor? Don't you think it is high time that we stir a little life into the slackness and sloppiness of halfheartedness and cowardliness?" This last speech now reads: "Well, what do you say to a little hypodermic for these fence-sitting deadheads?"

It was possible to peer into the original play with as clear an eye as one could who knew no Norwegian. There were no English sentences to correct and rewrite, only the bare literalness of the original. This version of the play, then, is really in the nature of a new translation into spoken English.

But it is more too. The original has a tendency to indulge in transitions between scenes that are themselves uninteresting, and although as little as possible of the original construction has been changed and the play is exactly as it was, scene for scene, I have made each act seem of one piece, instead of separate scenes. And my reason for doing this is simply that the tradition of Ibsen's theater allowed the opera-like separation of scenes, while ours demands that the audience never be conscious that a "scene" has taken place at all.

Structurally the largest change is in the third act—Ibsen's fifth. In the original the actual dramatic end comes a little past the middle of the act, but it is followed by a wind-up that keeps winding endlessly to the curtain. I think this overwriting was the result of Ibsen's insistence that his meaning be driven home—and from the front door right through to the back, lest the audience fail to understand him. Generally, in this act, I have brought out the meaning of the play in terms of dramatic action, action which was already there and didn't need to be newly invented, but which was separated by tendentious speeches spoken into the blue.

Throughout the play I have tried to peel away its trappings of the moment, its relatively accidental details which ring the dull green tones of Victorianism, and to show that beneath them there still lives the terrible wrath of Henrik Ibsen, who could make a play as men make watches, precisely, intelligently, and telling not merely the minute and the hour but the age.

AN ENEMY OF THE PEOPLE

AN ENEMY OF THE PEOPLE

Cast

OF THE ORIGINAL PRODUCTION OF THIS ADAPTATION,
IN ORDER OF APPEARANCE

MORTEN KIIL .... Art Smith
BILLING .... Michael Strong
MRS. STOCKMANN .... Florence Eldridge
PETER STOCKMANN .... Morris Carnovsky
HOVSTAD .... Martin Brooks
DR. STOCKMANN .... Fredric March
MORTEN .... Ralph Robertson
EJLIF .... Richard Trask
CAPTAIN HORSTER .... Ralph Dunn
PETRA .... Anna Minot
ASLAKSEN .... Fred Stewart
THE DRUNK .... Lou Gilbert
TOWNSPEOPLE: Lulla Adler, Barbara Ames, Paul Fitz-
   patrick, James Karen, Michael Lewin, Salem Lud-
   wig, Gene Lyons, John Marley, Arnold Schulman,
   Robert Simon, Rod Steiger

Production directed by Robert Lewis.
Setting and costumes by Aline Bernstein.
Lighting by Charles Elson.
*Presented by Lars Nordenson at the Broadhurst
Theatre in New York on December 28, 1950.*

AN ENEMY OF THE PEOPLE

Synopsis of Scenes

THE ACTION TAKES PLACE IN A NORWEGIAN TOWN

ACT ONE

Scene 1 : Dr. Stockmann's living room.
Scene 2 : The same, the following morning.

ACT TWO

Scene 1 : Editorial office of the *People's Daily Messenger*.
Scene 2 : A room in Captain Horster's house.

ACT THREE

Scene : Dr. Stockmann's living room the following morning.

*Throughout, in the stage directions, right and left
mean stage right and stage left.*

Act One: Scene 1

It is evening. Dr. Stockmann's living room is simply but cheer-fully furnished. A doorway, upstage right, leads into the en-trance hall, which extends from the front door to the dining room, running unseen behind the living room. At the left is another door, which leads to the Doctor's study and other rooms. In the upstage left corner is a stove. Toward the left foreground is a sofa with a table behind it. In the right fore-ground are two chairs, a small table between them, on which stand a lamp and a bowl of apples. At the back, to the left, an open doorway leads to the dining room, part of which is seen. The windows are in the right wall, a bench in front of them.

As the curtain rises, Billing and Morten Kiil are eating in the dining room. Billing is junior editor of the People's Daily Messenger. *Kiil is a slovenly old man who is feeding himself in a great hurry. He gulps his last bite and comes into the liv-ing room, where he puts on his coat and ratty fur hat. Billing comes in to help him.*

BILLING: You sure eat fast, Mr. Kiil. *Billing is an enthusiast to the point of foolishness.*

KIIL: Eating don't get you anywhere, boy. Tell my daughter I went home.

Kiil starts across to the front door. Billing returns to his food in the dining room. Kiil halts at the bowl of apples; he takes

17

one, tastes it, likes it, takes another and puts it in his pocket, then continues on toward the door. Again he stops, returns, and takes another apple for his pocket. Then he sees a to-bacco can on the table. He covers his action from Billing's possible glance, opens the can, smells it, pours some into his side pocket. He is just closing the can when Catherine Stock-mann enters from the dining room.

MRS. STOCKMANN: Father! You're not going, are you?

KIIL: Got business to tend to.

MRS. STOCKMANN: Oh, you're only going back to your room and you know it. Stay! Mr. Billing's here, and Hovstad's coming. It'll be interesting for you.

KIIL: Got all kinds of business. The only reason I came over was the butcher told me you bought roast beef today. Very tasty, dear.

MRS. STOCKMANN: Why don't you wait for Tom? He only went for a little walk.

KIIL, *taking out his pipe:* You think he'd mind if I filled my pipe?

MRS. STOCKMANN: No, go ahead. And here—take some apples. You should always have some fruit in your room.

KIIL: No, no, wouldn't think of it.

The doorbell rings.

MRS. STOCKMANN: That must be Hovstad. *She goes to the door and opens it.*

Peter Stockmann, the Mayor, enters. He is a bachelor, nearing sixty. He has always been one of those men who make it their life work to stand in the center of the ship to keep it from

18

overturning. He probably envies the family life and warmth of this house, but when he comes he never wants to admit he came and often sits with his coat on.

MRS. STOCKMANN: Peter! Well, this is a surprise!

PETER STOCKMANN: I was just passing by . . . *He sees Kiil and smiles, amused.* Mr. Kiil!

KIIL, *sarcastically:* Your Honor! *He bites into his apple and exits.*

MRS. STOCKMANN: You musn't mind him, Peter, he's getting terribly old. Would you like a bite to eat?

PETER STOCKMANN: No, no thanks. *He sees Billing now, and Billing nods to him from the dining room.*

MRS. STOCKMANN, *embarrassed:* He just happened to drop in.

PETER STOCKMANN: That's all right. I can't take hot food in the evening. Not with my stomach.

MRS. STOCKMANN: Can't I ever get you to eat anything in this house?

PETER STOCKMANN: Bless you, I stick to my tea and toast. Much healthier and more economical.

MRS. STOCKMANN, *smiling:* You sound as though Tom and I throw money out the window.

PETER STOCKMANN: Not you, Catherine. He wouldn't be home, would he?

MRS. STOCKMANN: He went for a little walk with the boys.

PETER STOCKMANN: You don't think that's dangerous, right after dinner? *There is a loud knocking on the front door. That* sounds like my brother.

MRS. STOCKMANN: I doubt it, so soon. Come in, please.

Hovstad enters. He is in his early thirties, a graduate of the peasantry struggling with a terrible conflict. For while he hates authority and wealth, he cannot bring himself to cast off a certain desire to partake of them. Perhaps he is dangerous because he wants more than anything to belong, and in a radical that is a withering wish, not easily to be borne.

MRS. STOCKMANN: Mr. Hovstad—

HOVSTAD: Sorry I'm late. I was held up at the printing shop. *Surprised:* Good evening, Your Honor.

PETER STOCKMANN, *rather stiffly:* Hovstad. On business, no doubt.

HOVSTAD: Partly. It's about an article for the paper—

PETER STOCKMANN, *sarcastically:* Ha! I don't doubt it. I understand my brother has become a prolific contributor to—what do you call it?—the *People's Daily Liberator?*

HOVSTAD, *laughing, but holding his ground:* The *People's Daily Messenger,* sir. The Doctor sometimes honors the *Messenger* when he wants to uncover the real truth of some subject.

PETER STOCKMANN: The truth! Oh, yes, I see.

MRS. STOCKMANN, *nervously to Hovstad:* Would you like to . . . *She points to dining room.*

PETER STOCKMANN: I don't want you to think I blame the Doctor for using your paper. After all, every performer goes for the audience that applauds him most. It's really not your paper I have anything against, Mr. Hovstad.

HOVSTAD: I really didn't think so, Your Honor.

Act One

PETER STOCKMANN: As a matter of fact, I happen to admire the spirit of tolerance in our town. It's magnificent. Just don't forget that we have it because we all believe in the same thing; it brings us together.

HOVSTAD: Kirsten Springs, you mean.

PETER STOCKMANN: The springs, Mr. Hovstad, our wonderful new springs. They've changed the soul of this town. Mark my words, Kirsten Springs are going to put us on the map, and there is no question about it.

MRS. STOCKMANN: That's what Tom says too.

PETER STOCKMANN: Everything is shooting ahead—real estate going up, money changing hands every hour, business humming—

HOVSTAD: And no more unemployment.

PETER STOCKMANN: Right. Give us a really good summer, and sick people will be coming here in carloads. The springs will turn into a regular fad, a new Carlsbad. And for once the well-to-do people won't be the only ones paying taxes in this town.

HOVSTAD: I hear reservations are really starting to come in?

PETER STOCKMANN: Coming in every day. Looks very promising, very promising.

HOVSTAD: That's fine. *To Mrs. Stockmann:* Then the Doctor's article will come in handy.

PETER STOCKMANN: He's written something again?

HOVSTAD: No, it's a piece he wrote at the beginning of the winter, recommending the water. But at the time I let the article lie.

PETER STOCKMANN: Why, some hitch in it?

HOVSTAD: Oh, no, I just thought it would have a bigger effect in the spring, when people start planning for the summer.

PETER STOCKMANN: That's smart, Mr. Hovstad, very smart.

MRS. STOCKMANN: Tom is always so full of ideas about the springs; every day he—

PETER STOCKMANN: Well, he ought to be, he gets his salary from the springs, my dear.

HOVSTAD: Oh, I think it's more than that, don't you? After all, Doctor Stockmann *created* Kirsten Springs.

PETER STOCKMANN: You don't say! I've been hearing that lately, but I did think I had a certain modest part—

MRS. STOCKMANN: Oh, Tom always says—

HOVSTAD: I only meant the original idea was—

PETER STOCKMANN: My good brother is never at a loss for ideas. All sorts of ideas. But when it comes to putting them into action you need another kind of man, and I did think that at least people in this house would—

MRS. STOCKMANN: But Peter, dear—we didn't mean to— Go get yourself a bite, Mr. Hovstad, my husband will be here any minute.

HOVSTAD: Thank you, maybe just a little something. *He goes into the dining room and joins Billing at the table.*

PETER STOCKMANN, *lowering his voice:* Isn't it remarkable? Why is it that people without background can never learn tact?

MRS. STOCKMANN: Why let it bother you? Can't you and Thomas share the honor like good brothers?

PETER STOCKMANN: The trouble is that certain men are never satisfied to share, Catherine.

MRS. STOCKMANN: Nonsense. You've always gotten along beautifully with Tom— That must be him now.

She goes to the front door, opens it. Dr. Stockmann is laughing and talking outside. He is in the prime of his life. He might be called the eternal amateur—a lover of things, of people, of sheer living, a man for whom the days are too short, and the future fabulous with discoverable joys. And for all this most people will not like him—he will not compromise for less than God's own share of the world while they have settled for less than Man's.

DR. STOCKMANN, *in the entrance hall:* Hey, Catherine! Here's another guest for you! Here's a hanger for your coat, Captain. Oh, that's right, you don't wear overcoats! Go on in, boys. You kids must be hungry all over again. Come here, Captain Horster, I want you to get a look at this roast. *He pushes Captain Horster along the hallway to the dining room. Ejlif and Morten also go to the dining room.*

MRS. STOCKMANN: Tom, dear . . . *She motions toward Peter in the living room.*

DR. STOCKMANN, *turns around in the doorway to the living room and sees Peter:* Oh, Peter . . . *He walks across and stretches out his hand.* Say now, this is really nice.

PETER STOCKMANN: I'll have to go in a minute.

DR. STOCKMANN: Oh, nonsense, not with the toddy on the table. You haven't forgotten the toddy, have you, Catherine?

MRS. STOCKMANN: Of course not, I've got the water boiling. *She goes into the dining room.*

PETER STOCKMANN: Toddy too?

DR. STOCKMANN: Sure, just sit down and make yourself at home.

PETER STOCKMANN: No, thanks, I don't go in for drinking parties.

DR. STOCKMANN: But this is no party.

PETER STOCKMANN: What else do you call it? *He looks toward the dining room.* It's extraordinary how you people can consume all this food and live.

DR. STOCKMANN, *rubbing his hands:* Why? What's finer than to watch young people eat? Peter, those are the fellows who are going to stir up the whole future.

PETER STOCKMANN, *a little alarmed:* Is that so! What's there to stir up? *He sits in a chair to the left.*

DR. STOCKMANN, *walking around:* Don't worry, they'll let us know when the time comes. Old idiots like you and me, we'll be left behind like—

PETER STOCKMANN: I've never been called *that* before.

DR. STOCKMANN: Oh, Peter, don't jump on me every minute! You know your trouble, Peter? Your impressions are blunted. You ought to sit up there in that crooked corner of the north for five years, the way I did, and then come back here. It's like watching the first seven days of creation!

PETER STOCKMANN: Here!

DR. STOCKMANN: Things to work and fight for, Peter! Without that you're dead. Catherine, you sure the mailman came today?

MRS. STOCKMANN, *from the dining room:* There wasn't any mail today.

DR. STOCKMANN: And another thing, Peter—a good income; *that's* something you learn to value after you've lived on a starvation diet.

PETER STOCKMANN: When did you starve?

DR. STOCKMANN: Damned near! It was pretty tough going a lot of the time up there. And now, to be able to live like a prince! Tonight, for instance, we had roast beef for dinner, and, by God, there was enough left for supper too. Please have a piece—come here.

PETER STOCKMANN: Oh, no, no—please, certainly not.

DR. STOCKMANN: At least let me show it to you! Come in here—we even have a tablecloth. *He pulls his brother toward the dining room.*

PETER STOCKMANN: I saw it.

DR. STOCKMANN: Live to the hilt! that's my motto. Anyway, Catherine says I'm earning almost as much as we spend.

PETER STOCKMANN, *refusing an apple:* Well, you are improving.

DR. STOCKMANN: Peter, that was a joke! You're supposed to laugh! *He sits in the other chair to the left.*

PETER STOCKMANN: Roast beef twice a day is no joke.

DR. STOCKMANN: Why can't I give myself the pleasure of having people around me? It's a necessity for me to see young, lively, happy people, free people burning with a desire to do something. You'll see. When Hovstad comes in we'll talk and—

PETER STOCKMANN: Oh, yes, Hovstad. That reminds me. He told me he was going to print one of your articles.

DR. STOCKMANN: One of my articles?

PETER STOCKMANN: Yes, about the springs—an article you wrote during the winter?

DR. STOCKMANN: Oh, that one! In the first place, I don't want that one printed right now.

PETER STOCKMANN: No? It sounded to me like it would be very timely.

DR. STOCKMANN: Under normal conditions, maybe so. *He gets up and walks across the floor.*

PETER STOCKMANN, *looking after him:* Well, what is abnormal about the conditions now?

DR. STOCKMANN, *stopping:* I can't say for the moment, Peter—at least not tonight. There could be a great deal abnormal about conditions; then again, there could be nothing at all.

PETER STOCKMANN: Well, you've managed to sound mysterious. Is there anything wrong? Something you're keeping from me? Because I wish once in a while you'd remind yourself that I am chairman of the board for the springs.

DR. STOCKMANN: And I would like *you* to remember that, Peter. Look, let's not get into each other's hair.

PETER STOCKMANN: I don't make a habit of getting into people's hair! But I'd like to underline that everything concerning Kirsten Springs must be treated in a businesslike manner, through the proper channels, and dealt with by the legally constituted authorities. I can't allow anything done behind my back in a roundabout way.

DR. STOCKMANN: When did I ever go behind your back, Peter?

PETER STOCKMANN: You have an ingrained tendency to go

your own way, Thomas, and that simply can't go on in a well-organized society. The individual really must subordinate himself to the over-all, or—*groping for words, he points to himself*—to the authorities who are in charge of the general welfare. *He gets up.*

DR. STOCKMANN: Well, that's probably so. But how the hell does that concern me, Peter?

PETER STOCKMANN: My dear Thomas, this is exactly what you will never learn. But you had better watch out because someday you might pay dearly for it. Now I've said it. Good-by.

DR. STOCKMANN: Are you out of your mind? You're absolutely on the wrong track.

PETER STOCKMANN: I am usually not. Anyway, may I be excused? *He nods toward the dining room.* Good-by, Catherine. Good evening, gentlemen. *He leaves.*

MRS. STOCKMANN, *entering the living room:* He left?

DR. STOCKMANN: And burned up!

MRS. STOCKMANN: What did you do to him now?

DR. STOCKMANN: What does he want from me? He can't expect me to give him an accounting of every move I make, every thought I think, until I am ready to do it.

MRS. STOCKMANN: Why? What should you give him an accounting of?

DR. STOCKMANN, *hesitantly:* Just leave that to me, Catherine. Peculiar the mailman didn't come today.

Hovstad, Billing, and Captain Horster have gotten up from the dining-room table and enter the living room. Ejlif and Morten come in a little later. Catherine exits.

BILLING, *stretching out his arms:* After a meal like that, by God, I feel like a new man. This house is so—

HOVSTAD, *cutting him off:* The Mayor certainly wasn't in a glowing mood tonight.

DR. STOCKMANN: It's his stomach. He has a lousy digestion.

HOVSTAD: I think two editors from the *People's Daily Messenger* didn't help either.

DR. STOCKMANN: No, it's just that Peter is a lonely man. Poor fellow, all he knows is official business and duties, and then all that damn weak tea that he pours into himself. Catherine, may we have the toddy?

MRS. STOCKMANN, *calling from the dining room:* I'm just getting it.

DR. STOCKMANN: Sit down here on the couch with me, Captain Horster—a rare guest like you—sit here. Sit down, friends.

HORSTER: This used to be such an ugly house. Suddenly it's beautiful!

Billing and Hovstad sit down at the right. Mrs. Stockmann brings a tray with pot, glasses, bottles, etc. on it, and puts it on the table behind the couch.

BILLING, *to Horster, intimately, indicating Stockmann:* Great man!

MRS. STOCKMANN: Here you are. Help yourselves.

DR. STOCKMANN, *taking a glass:* We sure will. *He mixes the toddy.* And the cigars, Ejlif—you know where the box is. And Morten, get my pipe. *The boys go out to the left.* I have a sneaking suspicion that Ejlif is snitching a cigar now and then, but I don't pay any attention. Catherine, you know where I put it? Oh, he's got it. Good boys! *The boys bring the various things in.* Help yourselves, fellows. I'll stick to the pipe. This one's gone through plenty of blizzards with me up in the north. Skol! *He looks around.* Home! What an invention, heh?

The boys sit down on the bench near the windows.

MRS. STOCKMANN, *who has sat down and is now knitting:* Are you sailing soon, Captain Horster?

HORSTER: I expect to be ready next week.

MRS. STOCKMANN: And then to America, Captain?

HORSTER: Yes, that's the plan.

BILLING: Oh, then you won't be home for the new election?

HORSTER: Is there going to be another election?

BILLING: Didn't you know?

HORSTER: No, I don't get mixed up in those things.

BILLING: But you are interested in public affairs, aren't you?

HORSTER: Frankly, I don't understand a thing about it.

He does, really, although not very much. Captain Horster is one of the longest silent roles in dramatic literature, but he is not to be thought of as characterless therefor. It is not a bad thing to have a courageous, quiet man for a friend, even if it has gone out of fashion.

MRS. STOCKMANN, *sympathetically:* Neither do I, Captain. Maybe that's why I'm always so glad to see you.

BILLING: Just the same, you ought to vote, Captain.

HORSTER: Even if I don't understand anything about it?

BILLING: Understand! What do you mean by that? Society, Captain, is like a ship—every man should do something to help navigate the ship.

HORSTER: That may be all right on shore, but on board a ship it doesn't work out so well.

Petra in hat and coat and with textbooks and notebooks under her arm comes into the entrance hall. She is Ibsen's clear-eyed hope for the future—and probably ours. She is forthright, determined, and knows the meaning of work, which to her is the creation of good on the earth.

PETRA, *from the hall:* Good evening.

DR. STOCKMANN, *warmly:* Good evening, Petra!

BILLING, *to Horster:* Great young woman!

There are mutual greetings. Petra removes her coat and hat and places the books on a chair in the entrance hall.

PETRA, *entering the living room:* And here you are, lying around like lizards while I'm out slaving.

DR. STOCKMANN: Well, you come and be a lizard too. Come here, Petra, sit with me. I look at her and say to myself, "How did I do it?"

Petra goes over to her father and kisses him.

BILLING: Shall I mix a toddy for you?

PETRA, *coming up to the table:* No, thanks, I had better do it myself—you always mix it too strong. Oh, Father, I forgot—I have a letter for you. *She goes to the chair where her books are.*

DR. STOCKMANN, *alerted:* Who's it from?

PETRA: I met the mailman on the way to school this morning

and he gave me your mail too, and I just didn't have time to run back.

DR. STOCKMANN, *getting up and walking toward her:* And you don't give it to me until now!

PETRA: I really didn't have time to run back, Father.

MRS. STOCKMANN: If she didn't have time . . .

DR. STOCKMANN: Let's see it—come on, child! *He takes the letter and looks at the envelope.* Yes, indeed.

MRS. STOCKMANN: Is that the one you've been waiting for?

DR. STOCKMANN: I'll be right back There wouldn't be a light on in my room, would there?

MRS. STOCKMANN: The lamp is on the desk, burning away.

DR. STOCKMANN: Please excuse me for a moment. *He goes into his study and quickly returns. Mrs. Stockmann hands him his glasses. He goes out again.*

PETRA: What is that, Mother?

MRS. STOCKMANN: I don't know. The last couple of days he's been asking again and again about the mailman.

BILLING: Probably an out-of-town patient of his.

PETRA: Poor Father, he's got much too much to do. *She mixes her drink.* This ought to taste good.

HOVSTAD: By the way, what happened to that English novel you were going to translate for us?

PETRA: I started it, but I've gotten so busy—

HOVSTAD: Oh, teaching evening school again?

PETRA: Two hours a night.

BILLING: Plus the high school every day?

PETRA, *sitting down on the couch:* Yes, five hours, and every night a pile of lessons to correct!

MRS. STOCKMANN: She never stops going.

HOVSTAD: Maybe that's why I always think of you as kind of breathless and—well, breathless.

PETRA: I love it. I get so wonderfully tired.

BILLING, *to Horster:* She looks tired.

MORTEN: You must be a wicked woman, Petra.

PETRA, *laughing:* Wicked?

MORTEN: You work so much. My teacher says that work is a punishment for our sins.

EJLIF: And you believe that?

MRS. STOCKMANN: Ejlif! Of course he believes his teacher!

BILLING, *smiling:* Don't stop him . . .

HOVSTAD: Don't you like to work, Morten?

MORTEN: Work? No.

HOVSTAD: Then what will you ever amount to in this world?

MORTEN: Me? I'm going to be a Viking.

EJLIF. You can't! You'd have to be a heathen!

MORTEN: So I'll be a heathen.

MRS. STOCKMANN: I think it's getting late, boys.

BILLING: I agree with you, Morten. I think—

MRS. STOCKMANN, *making signs to Billing:* You certainly don't, Mr. Billing.

BILLING: Yes, by God, I do. I am a real heathen and proud of it. You'll see, pretty soon we're all going to be heathens!

MORTEN: And then we can do anything we want!

BILLING: Right! You see, Morten—

MRS. STOCKMANN, *interrupting:* Don't you have any homework for tomorrow, boys? Better go in and do it.

EJLIF: Oh, can't we stay in here a while?

MRS. STOCKMANN: No, neither of you. Now run along.

The boys say good night and go off at the left.

HOVSTAD: You really think it hurts them to listen to such talk?

MRS. STOCKMANN: I don't know, but I don't like it.

Dr. Stockmann enters from his study, an open letter in his hand. He is like a sleepwalker, astonished, engrossed. He walks toward the front door.

MRS. STOCKMANN: Tom!

He turns, suddenly aware of them.

DR. STOCKMANN: Boys, there is going to be news in this town!

BILLING: News?

MRS STOCKMANN: What kind of news?

DR. STOCKMANN: A terrific discovery, Catherine.

HOVSTAD: Really?

MRS. STOCKMANN: That you made?

DR. STOCKMANN: That I made. *He walks back and forth.* Now

33

let the baboons running this town call me a lunatic! Now they'd better watch out. Oh, how the mighty have fallen!

PETRA: What is it, Father?

DR. STOCKMANN: Oh, if Peter were only here! Now you'll see how human beings can walk around and make judgments like blind rats.

HOVSTAD: What in the world's happened, Doctor?

DR. STOCKMANN, *stopping at the table:* It's the general opinion, isn't it, that our town is a sound and healthy spot?

HOVSTAD: Of course.

MRS. STOCKMANN: What happened?

DR. STOCKMANN: Even a rather unusually healthy spot! Oh, God, a place that can be recommended not only to all people but to sick people!

MRS. STOCKMANN: But, Tom, what are you—

DR. STOCKMANN: And we certainly have recommended it. I myself have written and written, in the *People's Messenger,* pamphlets—

HOVSTAD: Yes, yes, but—

DR. STOCKMANN: The miraculous springs that cost such a fortune to build, the whole Health Institute, is a pesthole!

PETRA: Father! The springs?

MRS. STOCKMANN, *simultaneously:* Our springs?

BILLING: That's unbelievable!

DR. STOCKMANN: You know the filth up in Windmill Valley? That stuff that has such a stinking smell? It comes down from the tannery up there, and the same damn poisonous mess comes right out into the blessed, miraculous water we're supposed to *cure* people with!

HORSTER: You mean actually where our beaches are?

DR. STOCKMANN: Exactly.

HOVSTAD: How are you so sure about this, Doctor?

DR. STOCKMANN: I had a suspicion about it a long time ago—last year there were too many sick cases among the visitors, typhoid and gastric disturbances.

MRS. STOCKMANN: That did happen. I remember Mrs. Svensen's niece—

DR. STOCKMANN: Yes, dear. At the time we thought that the visitors brought the bug, but later this winter I got a new idea and I started investigating the water.

MRS. STOCKMANN: So that's what you've been working on!

DR. STOCKMANN: I sent samples of the water to the University for an exact chemical analysis.

HOVSTAD: And that's what you have just received?

DR. STOCKMANN, *waving the letter again:* This is it. It proves the existence of infectious organic matter in the water.

MRS. STOCKMANN: Well, thank God you discovered it in time.

DR. STOCKMANN: I think we can say that, Catherine.

MRS. STOCKMANN: Isn't it wonderful!

HOVSTAD: And what do you intend to do now, Doctor?

DR. STOCKMANN: Put the thing right, of course.

HOVSTAD: Do you think that can be done?

DR. STOCKMANN: Maybe. If not, the whole Institute is useless. But there's nothing to worry about—I am quite clear on what has to be done.

MRS. STOCKMANN: But, Tom, why did you keep it so secret?

DR. STOCKMANN: What did you want me to do? Go out and shoot my mouth off before I really knew? *He walks around, rubbing his hands.* You don't realize what this means, Catherine—the whole water system has got to be changed.

MRS. STOCKMANN: The *whole* water system?

DR. STOCKMANN: The whole water system. The intake is too low, it's got to be raised to a much higher spot. The whole construction's got to be ripped out!

PETRA: Well, Father, at last you can prove they should have listened to you!

DR. STOCKMANN: Ha, she remembers!

MRS. STOCKMANN: That's right, you did warn them—

DR. STOCKMANN: Of course I warned them. When they started the damned thing I told them not to build it down there! But who am I, a mere scientist, to tell politicians where to build a health institute! Well, now they're going to get it, both barrels!

BILLING: This is tremendous! *To Horster:* He's a great man!

DR. STOCKMANN: It's bigger than tremendous. *He starts toward his study.* Wait'll they see this! *He stops.* Petra, my report is on my desk . . . *Petra goes into his study.* An envelope, Catherine! *She goes for it.* Gentlemen, this final proof from the University—*Petra comes out with the report, which he takes—*and my report—*he flicks the pages—*five solid, explosive pages . . .

MRS. STOCKMANN, *handing him an envelope:* Is this big enough?

DR. STOCKMANN: Fine. Right to the Board of Directors! *He inserts the report, seals the envelope, and hands it to Catherine.* Will you give this to the maid—what's her name again?

MRS. STOCKMANN: Randine, dear, Randine.

DR. STOCKMANN: Tell our darling Randine to wipe her nose and run over to the Mayor right now.

Mrs. Stockmann just stands there looking at him.

DR. STOCKMANN: What's the matter, dear?

MRS. STOCKMANN: I don't know . . .

PETRA: What's Uncle Peter going to say about this?

MRS. STOCKMANN: That's what I'm wondering.

DR. STOCKMANN: What can he say! He ought to be damn glad that such an important fact is brought out before we start an epidemic! Hurry, dear!

Catherine exits at the left.

HOVSTAD: I would like to put a brief item about this discovery in the *Messenger*.

DR. STOCKMANN: Go ahead. I'd really be grateful for that now.

HOVSTAD: Because the public ought to know soon.

DR. STOCKMANN: Right away.

BILLING: By God, you'll be the leading man in this town, Doctor.

DR. STOCKMANN, *walking around with an air of satisfaction:*

Oh, there was nothing to it. Every detective gets a lucky break once in his life. But just the same I—

BILLING: Hovstad, don't you think the town ought to pay Dr. Stockmann some tribute?

DR. STOCKMANN: Oh, no, no . . .

HOVSTAD: Sure, let's all put in a word for—

BILLING: I'll talk to Aslaksen about it!

Catherine enters.

DR. STOCKMANN: No, no, fellows, no fooling around! I won't put up with any commotion. Even if the Board of Directors wants to give me an increase I won't take it—I just won't take it, Catherine.

MRS. STOCKMANN, *dutifully:* That's right, Tom.

PETRA, *lifting her glass:* Skol, Father!

EVERYBODY: Skol, Doctor!

HORSTER: Doctor, I hope this will bring you great honor and pleasure.

DR. STOCKMANN: Thanks, friends, thanks. There's one blessing above all others. To have earned the respect of one's neighbors is—is— Catherine, I'm going to dance!

He grabs his wife and whirls her around. There are shouts and struggles, general commotion. The boys in nightgowns stick their heads through the doorway at the right, wondering what is going on. Mrs. Stockmann, seeing them, breaks away and chases them upstairs as

The Curtain Falls.

Act One: Scene 2

Dr. Stockmann's living room the following morning. As the curtain rises, Mrs. Stockmann comes in from the dining room, a sealed letter in her hand. She goes to the study door and peeks in.

MRS. STOCKMANN: Are you there, Tom?

DR. STOCKMANN, *from within*: I just got in. *He enters the living room.* What's up?

MRS. STOCKMANN: From Peter. It just came. *She hands him the envelope.*

DR. STOCKMANN: Oh, let's see. *He opens the letter and reads:* "I am returning herewith the report you submitted . . ." *He continues to read, mumbling to himself.*

MRS. STOCKMANN: Well, what does he say? Don't stand there!

DR. STOCKMANN, *putting the letter in his pocket:* He just says he'll come around this afternoon.

MRS. STOCKMANN: Oh. Well, maybe you ought to try to remember to be home then.

DR. STOCKMANN: Oh, I sure will. I'm through with my morning visits anyway.

MRS. STOCKMANN: I'm dying to see how he's going to take it.

DR. STOCKMANN: Why, is there any doubt? He'll probably make it look like he made the discovery, not I.

MRS. STOCKMANN: But aren't you a little bit afraid of that?

DR. STOCKMANN: Oh, underneath he'll be happy, Catherine. It's just that Peter is so afraid that somebody else is going to do something good for this town.

MRS. STOCKMANN: I wish you'd go out of your way and share the honors with him. Couldn't we say that he put you on the right track or something?

DR. STOCKMANN: Oh, I don't mind—as long as it makes everybody happy.

Morten Kiil sticks his head through the doorway. He looks around searchingly and chuckles. He will continue chuckling until he leaves the house. He is the archetype of the little twinkle-eyed man who sneaks into so much of Ibsen's work. He will chuckle you right over the precipice. He is the dealer, the man with the rat's finely tuned brain. But he is sometimes likable because he is without morals and announces the fact by laughing.

KIIL, *slyly:* Is it really true?

MRS. STOCKMANN, *walking toward him:* Father!

DR. STOCKMANN: Well, good morning!

MRS. STOCKMANN: Come on in.

KIIL: It better be true or I'm going.

DR. STOCKMANN: What had better be true?

KIIL: This crazy story about the water system. Is it true?

MRS. STOCKMANN: Of course it's true! How did you find out about it?

KIIL: Petra came flying by on her way to school this morning.

DR. STOCKMANN: Oh, she did?

KIIL: Ya. I thought she was trying to make a fool out of me—

MRS. STOCKMANN: Now why would she do that?

KIIL: Nothing gives more pleasure to young people than to make fools out of old people. But this is true, eh?

DR. STOCKMANN: Of course it's true. Sit down here. It's pretty lucky for the town, eh?

KIIL, *fighting his laughter:* Lucky for the town!

DR. STOCKMANN: I mean, that I made the discovery before it was too late.

KIIL: Tom, I never thought you had the imagination to pull your own brother's leg like this.

DR. STOCKMANN: Pull his leg?

MRS. STOCKMANN: But, Father, he's not—

KIIL: How does it go now, let me get it straight. There's some kind of—like cockroaches in the waterpipes—

DR. STOCKMANN, *laughing:* No, not cockroaches.

KIIL: Well, some kind of little animals.

MRS. STOCKMANN: Bacteria, Father.

KIIL, *who can barely speak through his laughter:* Ah, but a whole mess of them, eh?

DR. STOCKMANN: Oh, there'd be millions and millions.

KIIL: And nobody can see them but you, is that it?

DR. STOCKMANN: Yes, that's—well, of course anybody with a micro— *He breaks off*. What are you laughing at?

MRS. STOCKMANN, *smiling at Kiil:* You don't understand, Father. Nobody can actually see bacteria, but that doesn't mean they're not there.

KIIL: Good girl, you stick with him! By God, this is the best thing I ever heard in my life!

DR. STOCKMANN, *smiling:* What do you mean?

KIIL: But tell me, you think you are actually going to get your brother to believe this?

DR. STOCKMANN: Well, we'll see soon enough!

KIIL: You really think he's that crazy?

DR. STOCKMANN: I hope the whole town will be that crazy, Morten.

KIIL: Ya, they probably are, and it'll serve them right too—they think they're so much smarter than us old-timers. Your good brother ordered them to bounce me out of the council, so they chased me out like a dog! Make jackasses out of all of them, Stockmann!

DR. STOCKMANN: Yes, but, Morten—

KIIL: Long-eared, short-tailed jackasses! *He gets up*. Stockmann, if you can make the Mayor and his elegant friends grab at this bait, I will give a couple of hundred crowns to charity, and right now, right on the spot.

DR. STOCKMANN: Well, that would be very kind of you, but I'm—

KIIL: I haven't got much to play around with, but if you can

42

pull the rug out from under him with this cockroach business, I'll give at least fifty crowns to some poor people on Christmas Eve. Maybe this'll teach them to put some brains back in Town Hall!

Hovstad enters from the hall.

HOVSTAD: Good morning! Oh, pardon me . . .

KIIL, *enjoying this proof immensely:* Oh, this one is in on it, too?

HOVSTAD: What's that, sir?

DR. STOCKMANN: Of course he's in on it.

KIIL: Couldn't I have guessed that! And it's going to be in the papers, I suppose. You're sure tying down the corners, aren't you? Well, lay it on thick. I've got to go.

DR. STOCKMANN: Oh, no, stay a while, let me explain it to you!

KIIL: Oh, I get it, don't worry! Only you can see them, heh? That's the best idea I've ever—damn it, you shouldn't do this for nothing! *He goes toward the hall.*

MRS. STOCKMANN, *following him out, laughing:* But, Father, you don't understand about bacteria.

DR. STOCKMANN, *laughing:* The old badger doesn't believe a word of it.

HOVSTAD: What does he think you're doing?

DR. STOCKMANN: Making an idiot out of my brother—imagine that?

HOVSTAD: You got a few minutes?

DR. STOCKMANN: Sure, as long as you like.

HOVSTAD: Have you heard from the Mayor?

DR. STOCKMANN: Only that he's coming over later.

HOVSTAD: I've been thinking about this since last night—

DR. STOCKMANN: Don't say?

HOVSTAD: For you as a medical man, a scientist, this is a really rare opportunity. But I've been wondering if you realize that it ties in with a lot of other things.

DR. STOCKMANN: How do you mean? Sit down. *They sit at the right.* What are you driving at?

HOVSTAD: You said last night that the pollution comes from impurities in the ground—

DR. STOCKMANN: It comes from the poisonous dump up in Windmill Valley.

HOVSTAD: Doctor, I think it comes from an entirely different dump.

DR. STOCKMANN: What do you mean?

HOVSTAD, *with growing zeal:* The same dump that is poisoning and polluting our whole social life in this town.

DR. STOCKMANN: For God's sake, Hovstad, what are you babbling about?

HOVSTAD: Everything that matters in this town has fallen into the hands of a few bureaucrats.

DR. STOCKMANN: Well, they're not all bureaucrats—

HOVSTAD: They're all rich, all with old reputable names, and they've got everything in the palm of their hands.

DR. STOCKMANN: Yes, but they happen to have ability and knowledge.

HOVSTAD: Did they show ability and knowledge when they built the water system where they did?

DR. STOCKMANN: No, of course not, but that happened to be a blunder, and we'll clear it up now.

HOVSTAD: You really imagine it's going to be as easy as all that?

DR. STOCKMANN: Easy or not easy, it's got to be done.

HOVSTAD: Doctor, I've made up my mind to give this whole scandal very special treatment.

DR. STOCKMANN: Now wait. You can't call it a scandal yet.

HOVSTAD: Doctor, when I took over the *People's Messenger* I swore I'd blow that smug cabal of old, stubborn, self-satisfied fogies to bits. This is the story that can do it.

DR. STOCKMANN: But I still think we owe them a deep debt of gratitude for building the springs.

HOVSTAD: The Mayor being your brother, I wouldn't ordinarily want to touch it, but I know you'd never let that kind of thing obstruct the truth.

DR. STOCKMANN: Of course not, but . . .

HOVSTAD: I want you to understand me. I don't have to tell you I come from a simple family. I know in my bones what the underdog needs—he's got to have a say in the government of society. That's what brings out ability, intelligence, and self-respect in people.

DR. STOCKMANN: I understand that, but . . .

HOVSTAD: I think a newspaperman who turns down any chance to give the underdog a lift is taking on a responsibility that I don't want. I know perfectly well that in fancy circles they call it agitation, and they can call it anything they like if it makes them happy, but I have my own conscience—

DR. STOCKMANN, *interrupting:* I agree with you, Hovstad, but this is just the water supply and— *There is a knock on the door.* Damn it! Come in!

Mr. Aslaksen, the publisher, enters from the hall. He is simply but neatly dressed. He wears gloves and carries a hat and an umbrella in his hand. He is so utterly drawn it is unnecessary to say anything at all about him.

ASLAKSEN: I beg your pardon, Doctor, if I intrude . . .

HOVSTAD, *standing up:* Are you looking for me, Aslaksen?

ASLAKSEN: No, I didn't know you were here. I want to see the Doctor.

DR. STOCKMANN: What can I do for you?

ASLAKSEN: Is it true, Doctor, what I hear from Mr. Billing, that you intend to campaign for a better water system?

DR. STOCKMANN: Yes, for the Institute. But it's not a campaign.

ASLAKSEN: I just wanted to call and tell you that we are behind you a hundred per cent.

HOVSTAD, *to Dr. Stockmann:* There, you see!

DR. STOCKMANN: Mr. Aslaksen, I thank you with all my heart. But you see—

ASLAKSEN: We can be important, Doctor. When the little businessman wants to push something through, he turns out to be the majority, you know, and it's always good to have the majority on your side.

DR. STOCKMANN: That's certainly true, but I don't understand what this is all about. It seems to me it's a simple, straightforward business. The water—

ASLAKSEN: Of course we intend to behave with moderation, Doctor. I always try to be a moderate and careful man.

DR. STOCKMANN: You are known for that, Mr. Aslaksen, but—

ASLAKSEN: The water system is very important to us little businessmen, Doctor. Kirsten Springs are becoming a gold mine for this town, especially for the property owners, and that is why, in my capacity as chairman of the Property Owners Association—

DR. STOCKMANN: Yes.

ASLAKSEN: And furthermore, as a representative of the Temperance Society— You probably know, Doctor, that I am active for prohibition.

DR. STOCKMANN: So I have heard.

ASLAKSEN: As a result, I come into contact with all kinds of people, and since I am known to be a law-abiding and solid citizen, I have a certain influence in this town—you might even call it a little power.

DR. STOCKMANN: I know that very well, Mr. Aslaksen.

ASLAKSEN: That's why you can see that it would be practically nothing for me to arrange a demonstration.

DR. STOCKMANN: Demonstration! What are you going to demonstrate about?

ASLAKSEN: The citizens of the town complimenting you for bringing this important matter to everybody's attention. Obviously it would have to be done with the utmost moderation so as not to hurt the authorities.

HOVSTAD: This could knock the big-bellies right into the garbage can!

ASLAKSEN: No indiscretion or extreme aggressiveness toward the authorities, Mr. Hovstad! I don't want any wild-eyed radicalism on this thing. I've had enough of that in my time, and no good ever comes of it. But for a good solid citizen to express his calm, frank, and free opinion is something nobody can deny.

DR. STOCKMANN, *shaking the publisher's hand:* My dear Aslaksen, I can't tell you how it heartens me to hear this kind of support. I am happy—I really am—I'm happy. Listen! Wouldn't you like a glass of sherry?

ASLAKSEN: I am a member of the Temperance Society. I—

DR. STOCKMANN: Well, how about a glass of beer?

ASLAKSEN, *considers, then:* I don't think I can go quite that far, Doctor. I never take anything. Well, good day, and I want you to remember that the little man is behind you like a wall.

DR. STOCKMANN: Thank you.

ASLAKSEN: You have the solid majority on your side, because when the little—

DR. STOCKMANN, *trying to stop Aslaksen's talk:* Thanks for that, Mr. Aslaksen, and good day.

ASLAKSEN: Are you going back to the printing shop, Mr. Hovstad?

HOVSTAD: I just have a thing or two to attend to here.

ASLAKSEN: Very well. *He leaves.*

HOVSTAD: Well, what do you say to a little hypodermic for these fence-sitting deadheads?

DR. STOCKMANN, *surprised:* Why? I think Aslaksen is a very sincere man.

HOVSTAD: Isn't it time we pumped some guts into these well-intentioned men of good will? Under all their liberal talk they still idolize authority, and that's got to be rooted out of this town. This blunder of the water system has to be made clear to every voter. Let me print your report.

DR. STOCKMANN: Not until I talk to my brother.

HOVSTAD: I'll write an editorial in the meantime, and if the Mayor won't go along with us—

DR. STOCKMANN: I don't see how you can imagine such a thing!

HOVSTAD: Believe me, Doctor, it's possible, and then—

DR. STOCKMANN: Listen, I promise you: he will go along, and then you can print my report, every word of it.

HOVSTAD: On your word of honor?

DR. STOCKMANN, *giving Hovstad the manuscript:* Here it is. Take it. It can't do any harm for you to read it. Return it to me later.

HOVSTAD: Good day, Doctor.

DR. STOCKMANN: Good day. You'll see, it's going to be easier than you think, Hovstad!

HOVSTAD: I hope so, Doctor. Sincerely. Let me know as soon as you hear from His Honor. *He leaves.*

DR. STOCKMANN, *goes to dining room and looks in:* Catherine! Oh, you're home already, Petra!

PETRA, *coming in:* I just got back from school.

MRS. STOCKMANN, *entering:* Hasn't he been here yet?

DR. STOCKMANN: Peter? No, but I just had a long chat with Hovstad. He's really fascinated with my discovery, and you know, it has more implications that I thought at first. Do you know what I have backing me up?

MRS. STOCKMANN: What in heaven's name have you got backing you up?

DR. STOCKMANN: The solid majority.

MRS. STOCKMANN: Is that good?

DR. STOCKMANN: Good? It's wonderful. You can't imagine the feeling, Catherine, to know that your own town feels like a brother to you. I have never felt so at home in this town since I was a boy. *A noise is heard.*

MRS. STOCKMANN: That must be the front door.

DR. STOCKMANN: Oh, it's Peter then. Come in.

PETER STOCKMANN, *entering from the hall:* Good morning!

DR. STOCKMANN: It's nice to see you, Peter.

MRS. STOCKMANN: Good morning. How are you today?

PETER STOCKMANN: Well, so so. *To Dr. Stockmann:* I received your thesis about the condition of the springs yesterday.

DR. STOCKMANN: I got your note. Did you read it?

PETER STOCKMANN: I read it.

DR. STOCKMANN: Well, what do you have to say?

Peter Stockmann clears his throat and glances at the women.

MRS. STOCKMANN: Come on, Petra. *She and Petra leave the room at the left.*

PETER STOCKMANN, *after a moment:* Thomas, was it really necessary to go into this investigation behind my back?

DR. STOCKMANN: Yes. Until I was convinced myself, there was no point in—

PETER STOCKMANN: And now you are convinced?

DR. STOCKMANN: Well, certainly. Aren't you too, Peter? *Pause.* The University chemists corroborated . . .

PETER STOCKMANN: You intend to present this document to the Board of Directors, officially, as the medical officer of the springs?

DR. STOCKMANN: Of course, something's got to be done, and quick.

PETER STOCKMANN: You always use such strong expressions, Thomas. Among other things, in your report you say that we *guarantee* our guests and visitors a permanent case of poisoning.

DR. STOCKMANN: But, Peter, how can you describe it any other way? Imagine! Poisoned internally and externally!

PETER STOCKMANN: So you merrily conclude that we must build a waste-disposal plant—and reconstruct a brand-new water system from the bottom up!

DR. STOCKMANN: Well, do you know some other way out? I don't.

PETER STOCKMANN: I took a little walk over to the city engineer this morning and in the course of conversation I sort of jokingly mentioned these changes—as something we might consider for the future, you know.

DR. STOCKMANN: The future won't be soon enough, Peter.

PETER STOCKMANN: The engineer kind of smiled at my extravagance and gave me a few facts. I don't suppose you have taken the trouble to consider what your proposed changes would cost?

DR. STOCKMANN: No, I never thought of that.

PETER STOCKMANN: Naturally. Your little project would come to at least three hundred thousand crowns.

DR. STOCKMANN, *astonished:* That expensive!

PETER STOCKMANN: Oh, don't look so upset—it's only money. The worst thing is that it would take some two years.

DR. STOCKMANN: Two years?

PETER STOCKMANN: At the least. And what do you propose we do about the springs in the meantime? Shut them up, no doubt! Because we would have to, you know. As soon as the rumor gets around that the water is dangerous, we won't have a visitor left. So that's the picture, Thomas. You have it in your power literally to ruin your own town.

DR. STOCKMANN: Now look, Peter! I don't want to ruin anything.

PETER STOCKMANN: Kirsten Springs are the blood supply of this town, Thomas—the only future we've got here. Now will you stop and think?

DR. STOCKMANN: Good God! Well, what do you think we ought to do?

PETER STOCKMANN: Your report has not convinced me that the conditions are as dangerous as you try to make them.

DR. STOCKMANN: Now listen; they are even worse than the report makes them out to be. Remember, summer is coming, and the warm weather!

PETER STOCKMANN: I think you're exaggerating. A capable physician ought to know what precautions to take.

DR. STOCKMANN: And what then?

PETER STOCKMANN: The existing water supply for the springs is a fact, Thomas, and has got to be treated as a fact. If you are reasonable and act with discretion, the directors of the Institute will be inclined to take under consideration any means to make possible improvements, reasonably and without financial sacrifices.

DR. STOCKMANN: Peter, do you imagine that I would ever agree to such trickery?

PETER STOCKMANN: Trickery?

DR. STOCKMANN: Yes, a trick, a fraud, a lie! A treachery, a downright crime, against the public and against the whole community!

PETER STOCKMANN: I said before that I am not convinced that there is any actual danger.

DR. STOCKMANN: Oh, you aren't? Anything else is impossible! My report is an absolute fact. The only trouble is that you and your administration were the ones who insisted that the water supply be built where it is, and now you're afraid to admit the blunder you committed. Damn it! Don't you think I can see through it all?

PETER STOCKMANN: All right, let's suppose that's true. Maybe I do care a little about my reputation. I still say I do it for the good of the town—without moral authority there can be no government. And that is why, Thomas, it is my duty to prevent your report from reaching the Board. Some time later I will bring up the matter for discussion. In the meantime, not a single word is to reach the public.

DR. STOCKMANN: Oh, my dear Peter, do you imagine you can prevent that!

PETER STOCKMANN: It will be prevented.

DR. STOCKMANN: It can't be. There are too many people who already know about it.

PETER STOCKMANN, *angered:* Who? It can't possibly be those people from the *Daily Messenger* who—

DR. STOCKMANN: Exactly. The liberal, free, and independent press will stand up and do its duty!

PETER STOCKMANN: You are an unbelievably irresponsible man, Thomas! Can't you imagine what consequences that is going to have for you?

DR. STOCKMANN: For me?

PETER STOCKMANN: Yes, for you and your family.

DR. STOCKMANN: What the hell are you saying now!

PETER STOCKMANN: I believe I have the right to think of myself as a helpful brother, Thomas.

DR. STOCKMANN: You have been, and I thank you deeply for it.

PETER STOCKMANN: Don't mention it. I often couldn't help

54

myself. I had hoped that by improving your finances I would be able to keep you from running completely hog wild.

DR. STOCKMANN: You mean it was only for your own sake?

PETER STOCKMANN: Partly, yes. What do you imagine people think of an official whose closest relatives get themselves into trouble time and time again?

DR. STOCKMANN: And that's what I have done?

PETER STOCKMANN: You do it without knowing it. You're like a man with an automatic brain—as soon as an idea breaks into your head, no matter how idiotic it may be, you get up like a sleepwalker and start writing a pamphlet about it.

DR. STOCKMANN: Peter, don't you think it's a citizen's duty to share a new idea with the public?

PETER STOCKMANN: The public doesn't need new ideas—the public is much better off with old ideas.

DR. STOCKMANN: You're not even embarrassed to say that?

PETER STOCKMANN: Now look, I'm going to lay this out once and for all. You're always barking about authority. If a man gives you an order he's persecuting you. Nothing is important enough to respect once you decide to revolt against your superiors. All right then, I give up. I'm not going to try to change you any more. I told you the stakes you are playing for here, and now I am going to give you an order. And I warn you, you had better obey it if you value your career.

DR. STOCKMANN: What kind of an order?

PETER STOCKMANN: You are going to deny these rumors officially.

DR. STOCKMANN: How?

PETER STOCKMANN: You simply say that you went into the examination of the water more thoroughly and you find that you overestimated the danger.

DR. STOCKMANN: I see.

PETER STOCKMANN: And that you have complete confidence that whatever improvements are needed, the management will certainly take care of them.

DR. STOCKMANN, *after a pause:* My convictions come from the condition of the water. My convictions will change when the water changes, and for no other reason.

PETER STOCKMANN: What are you talking about convictions? You're an official, you keep your convictions to yourself!

DR. STOCKMANN: To myself?

PETER STOCKMANN: As an official, I said. God knows, as a private person that's something else, but as a subordinate employee of the Institute, you have no right to express any convictions or personal opinions about anything connected with policy.

DR. STOCKMANN: Now you listen to me. I am a doctor and a scientist—

PETER STOCKMANN: This has nothing to do with science!

DR. STOCKMANN: Peter, I have the right to express my opinion on anything in the world!

PETER STOCKMANN: Not about the Institute—that I forbid.

DR. STOCKMANN: You forbid!

PETER STOCKMANN: I forbid you as your superior, and when I give orders you obey.

DR. STOCKMANN: Peter, if you weren't my brother—

PETRA, *throwing the door at the left open:* Father! You aren't going to stand for this! *She enters.*

MRS. STOCKMANN, *coming in after her:* Petra, Petra!

PETER STOCKMANN: What have you two been doing, eavesdropping?

MRS. STOCKMANN: You were talking so loud we couldn't help . . .

PETRA: Yes, I was eavesdropping!

PETER STOCKMANN: That makes me very happy.

DR. STOCKMANN, *approaching his brother:* You said something to me about forbidding—

PETER STOCKMANN: You forced me to.

DR. STOCKMANN: So you want me to spit in my own face officially—is that it?

PETER STOCKMANN: Why must you always be so colorful?

DR. STOCKMANN: And if I don't obey?

PETER STOCKMANN: Then we will publish our own statement, to calm the public.

DR. STOCKMANN: Good enough! And I will write against you. I will stick to what I said, and I will prove that I am right and that you are wrong, and what will you do then?

PETER STOCKMANN: Then I simply won't be able to prevent your dismissal.

DR. STOCKMANN: What!

PETRA: Father!

PETER STOCKMANN: Dismissed from the Institute is what I said. If you want to make war on Kirsten Springs, you have no right to be on the Board of Directors.

DR. STOCKMANN, *after a pause:* You'd dare to do that?

PETER STOCKMANN: Oh, no, you're the daring man.

PETRA: Uncle, this is a rotten way to treat a man like Father!

MRS. STOCKMANN: Will you be quiet, Petra!

PETER STOCKMANN: So young and you've got opinions already —but that's natural. *To Mrs. Stockmann:* Catherine dear, you're probably the only sane person in this house. Knock some sense into his head, will you? Make him realize what he's driving his whole family into.

DR. STOCKMANN: My family concerns nobody but myself.

PETER STOCKMANN: His family and his own town.

DR. STOCKMANN: I'm going to show you who loves his town. The people are going to get the full stink of this corruption, Peter, and then we will see who loves his town!

PETER STOCKMANN: You love your town when you blindly, spitefully, stubbornly go ahead trying to cut off our most important industry?

DR. STOCKMANN: That source is poisoned, man. We are getting fat by peddling filth and corruption to innocent people!

PETER STOCKMANN: I think this has gone beyond opinions and convictions, Thomas. A man who can throw that kind of insinuation around is nothing but a traitor to society!

DR. STOCKMANN, *starting toward his brother in a fury:* How dare you to—

MRS. STOCKMANN, *stepping between them:* Tom!

PETRA, *grabbing her father's arm:* Be careful, Father!

PETER STOCKMANN, *with dignity:* I won't expose myself to violence. You have been warned. Consider what you owe yourself and your family! Good day! *He exits.*

DR. STOCKMANN, *walking up and down:* He's insulted. *He's* insulted!

MRS. STOCKMANN: It's shameful, Tom.

PETRA: Oh, I would love to give him a piece of my mind!

DR. STOCKMANN: It was my own fault! I should have shown my teeth right from the beginning. He called me a traitor to society. Me! Damn it all, that's not going to stick!

MRS. STOCKMANN: Please, think! He's got all the power on his side.

DR. STOCKMANN: Yes, but I have the truth on mine.

MRS. STOCKMANN: Without power, what good is the truth?

PETRA: Mother, how can you say such a thing?

DR. STOCKMANN: That's ridiculous, Catherine. I have the liberal press with me, and the majority. If that isn't power, what is?

MRS. STOCKMANN: But, for heaven's sake, Tom, you aren't going to—

DR. STOCKMANN: What am I not going to do?

MRS. STOCKMANN: You aren't going to fight it out in public with your brother!

DR. STOCKMANN: What the hell else do you want me to do?

MRS. STOCKMANN: But it won't do you any earthly good. If they won't do it, they won't. All you'll get out of it is a notice that you're fired.

DR. STOCKMANN: I am going to do my duty, Catherine. Me, the man he calls a traitor to society!

MRS. STOCKMANN: And how about your duty toward your family—the people you're supposed to provide for?

PETRA: Don't always think of us first, Mother.

MRS. STOCKMANN, *to Petra:* You can talk! If worst comes to worst, you can manage for yourself. But what about the boys, Tom, and you and me?

DR. STOCKMANN: What about you? You want me to be the miserable animal who'd crawl up the boots of that damn gang? Will you be happy if I can't face myself the rest of my life?

MRS. STOCKMANN: Tom, Tom, there's so much injustice in the world! You've simply got to learn to live with it. If you go on this way, God help us, we'll have no money again. Is it so long since the north that you've forgotten what it was to live like we lived? Haven't we had enough of that for one lifetime? *The boys enter.* What will happen to them? We've got nothing if you're fired!

DR. STOCKMANN: Stop it! *He looks at the boys.* Well, boys, did you learn anything in school today?

MORTEN, *looking at them, puzzled:* We learned what an insect is.

DR. STOCKMANN: You don't say!

MORTEN: What happened here? Why is everybody—

DR. STOCKMANN: Nothing, nothing. You know what I'm going to do, boys? From now on I'm going to teach you what a man is. *He looks at Mrs. Stockmann. She cries as*

The Curtain Falls.

Act Two: Scene 1

The editorial office of the People's Daily Messenger. *At the back of the room, to the left, is a door leading to the printing room. Near it, in the left wall, is another door. At the right of the stage is the entrance door. In the middle of the room there is a large table covered with papers, newspapers, and books. Around it are a few chairs. A writing desk stands against the right wall. The room is dingy and cheerless, the furniture shabby.*

As the curtain rises, Billing is sitting at the desk, reading the manuscript. Hovstad comes in after a moment from the printing room. Billing looks up.

BILLING: The Doctor not come yet?

HOVSTAD: No, not yet. You finish it?

Billing holds up a hand to signal "just a moment." He reads on, the last paragraph of the manuscript. Hovstad comes and stands over him, reading with him. Now Billing closes the manuscript, glances up at Hovstad with some trepidation, then looks off. Hovstad, looking at Billing, walks a few steps away.

HOVSTAD: Well? What do you think of it?

BILLING, *with some hesitation:* It's devastating. The Doctor is a brilliant man. I swear, I myself never really understood how incompetent those fat fellows are, on top. *He picks up the manuscript and waves it a little.* I hear the rumble of revolution in this.

HOVSTAD, *looking toward the door:* Sssh! Aslaksen's inside.

BILLING: Aslaksen's a coward. With all that moderation talk, all he's saying is, he's yellow. You're going to print this, aren't you?

HOVSTAD: Sure, I'm just waiting for the Doctor to give the word. If his brother hasn't given in, we put it on the press anyway.

BILLING: Yes, but if the Mayor's against this it's going to get pretty rough. You know that, don't you?

HOVSTAD: Just let him try to block the reconstruction—the little businessmen and the whole town'll be screaming for his head. Aslaksen'll see to that.

BILLING, *ecstatically:* The stockholders'll have to lay out a fortune of money if this goes through!

HOVSTAD: My boy, I think it's going to bust them. And when the springs go busted, the people are finally going to understand the level of genius that's been running this town. Those five sheets of paper are going to put in a liberal administration once and for all.

BILLING: It's a revolution. You know that? *With hope and fear:* I mean it, we're on the edge of a real revolution!

DR. STOCKMANN, *entering:* Put it on the press!

HOVSTAD, *excited:* Wonderful! What did the Mayor say?

DR. STOCKMANN: The Mayor has declared war, so war is what

it's going to be! *He takes the manuscript from Billing.* And this is only the beginning! You know what he tried to do?

BILLING, *calling into the printing room:* Mr. Aslaksen, the Doctor's here!

DR. STOCKMANN, *continuing:* He actually tried to blackmail me! He's got the nerve to tell me that I'm not allowed to speak my mind without his permission! Imagine the shameless effrontery!

HOVSTAD: He actually said it right out?

'DR. STOCKMANN: Right to my face! The trouble with me was I kept giving them credit for being our kind of people, but they're dictators! They're people who'll try to hold power even if they have to poison the town to do it.

Toward the last part of Dr. Stockmann's speech Aslaksen enters.

ASLAKSEN: Now take it easy, Doctor, you—you mustn't always be throwing accusations. I'm with you, you understand, but moderation—

DR. STOCKMANN, *cutting him off:* What'd you think of the article, Hovstad?

HOVSTAD: It's a masterpiece. In one blow you've managed to prove beyond any doubt what kind of men are running us.

ASLAKSEN: May we print it now, then?

DR. STOCKMANN: I should say *so!*

HOVSTAD: We'll have it ready for tomorrow's paper.

DR. STOCKMANN: And listen, Mr. Aslaksen, do me a favor, will you? You run a fine paper, but supervise the printing personally, eh? I'd hate to see the weather report stuck into the middle of my article.

ASLAKSEN, *laughing:* Don't worry, that won't happen this time!

DR. STOCKMANN: Make it perfect, eh? Like you were printing money. You can't imagine how I'm dying to see it in print. After all the lies in the papers, the half-lies, the quarter-lies—to finally see the absolute, unvarnished truth about something important. And this is only the beginning. We'll go on to other subjects and blow up every lie we live by! What do you say, Aslaksen?

ASLAKSEN, *nodding in agreement:* But just remember . . .

BILLING *and* HOVSTAD *together with* ASLAKSEN: Moderation!

ASLAKSEN, *to Billing and Hovstad:* I don't know what's so funny about that!

BILLING, *enthralled:* Doctor Stockmann, I feel as though I were standing in some historic painting. Goddammit, this is a historic day! Someday this scene'll be in a museum, entitled, "The Day the Truth Was Born."

DR. STOCKMANN, *suddenly:* Oh! I've got a patient half-bandaged down the street. *He leaves.*

HOVSTAD, *to Aslaksen:* I hope you realize how useful he could be to us.

ASLAKSEN: I don't like that business about "this is only the beginning." Let him stick to the springs.

BILLING: What makes you so scared all the time?

ASLAKSEN: I have to live here. It'd be different if he were attacking the national government or something, but if he thinks I'm going to start going after the whole town administration—

BILLING: What's the difference? Bad is bad!

ASLAKSEN: Yes, but there is a difference. You attack the national government, what's going to happen? Nothing. They go right on. But a town administration—they're liable to be overthrown or something! I represent the small property owners in this town—

BILLING: Ha! It's always the same. Give a man a little property and the truth can go to hell!

ASLAKSEN: Mr. Billing, I'm older than you are. I've seen fire-eaters before. You know who used to work at that desk before you? Councilman Stensford—*councilman!*

BILLING: Just because I work at a renegade's desk, does that mean—

ASLAKSEN: You're a politician. A politician never knows where he's going to end up. And besides you applied for a job as secretary to the Magistrate, didn't you?

HOVSTAD, *surprised, laughs:* Billing!

BILLING, *to Hovstad:* Well, why not? If I get it I'll have a chance to put across some good things. I could put plenty of big boys on the spot with a job like that!

ASLAKSEN: All right, I'm just saying. *He goes to the printing-room door.* People change. Just remember when you call me a coward—I may not have made the hot speeches, but I never went back on my beliefs either. Unlike some of the big radicals around here, I didn't change. Of course, I *am* a little more moderate, but moderation is—

HOVSTAD: Oh, God!

ASLAKSEN: I don't see what's so funny about that! *He glares at Hovstad and goes out.*

BILLING: If we could get rid of him we—

HOVSTAD: Take it easy—he pays the printing bill, he's not that bad. *He picks up the manuscript.* I'll get the printer on this. *He starts out.*

BILLING: Say, Hovstad, how about asking Stockmann to back us? Then we could really put out a paper!

HOVSTAD: What would he do for money?

BILLING: His father-in-law.

HOVSTAD: Kiil? Since when has he got money?

BILLING: I think he's loaded with it.

HOVSTAD: No! Why, as long as I've known him he's worn the same overcoat, the same suit—

BILLING: Yeah, and the same ring on his right hand. You ever get a look at that boulder? *He points to his finger.*

HOVSTAD: No, I never—

BILLING: All year he wears the diamond inside, but on New Year's Eve he turns it around. Figure it out—when a man has no visible means of support, what is he living on? Money, right?

Petra enters, carrying a book.

PETRA: Hello.

HOVSTAD: Well, fancy seeing you here. Sit down. What—

PETRA, *walking slowly up to Hovstad:* I want to ask you a question. *She starts to open the book.*

BILLING: What's that?

PETRA: The English novel you wanted translated.

HOVSTAD: Aren't you going to do it?

PETRA, *with deadly seriousness and curiosity:* I don't get this.

HOVSTAD: You don't get what?

PETRA: This book is absolutely against everything you people believe.

HOVSTAD: Oh, it isn't that bad.

PETRA: But, Mr. Hovstad, it says if you're good there's a supernatural force that'll fix it so you end up happy. And if you're bad you'll be punished. Since when does the world work that way?

HOVSTAD: Yes, Petra, but this is a newspaper, people like to read that kind of thing. They buy the paper for that and then we slip in our political stuff. A newspaper can't buck the public—

PETRA, *astonished, beginning to be angry:* You don't say! *She starts to go.*

HOVSTAD, *hurrying after her:* Now, wait a minute, I don't want you to go feeling that way. *He holds the manuscript out to Billing.* Here, take this to the printer, will you?

BILLING, *taking the manuscript:* Sure. *He goes.*

HOVSTAD: I just want you to understand something: I never even read that book. It was Billing's idea.

PETRA, *trying to penetrate his eyes:* I thought he was a radical.

HOVSTAD: He is. But he's also a—

PETRA, *testily:* A newspaperman.

HOVSTAD: Well, that too, but I was going to say that Billing is trying to get the job as secretary to the Magistrate.

PETRA: What?

HOVSTAD: People are—people, Miss Stockmann.

PETRA: But the Magistrate! He's been fighting everything progressive in this town for thirty years.

HOVSTAD: Let's not argue about it, I just didn't want you to go out of here with a wrong idea of me. I guess you know that I—I happen to admire women like you. I've never had a chance to tell you, but I—well, I want you to know it. Do you mind? *He smiles.*

PETRA: No, I don't mind, but—reading that book upset me. I really don't understand. Will you tell me why you're supporting my father?

HOVSTAD: What's the mystery? It's a matter of principle.

PETRA: But a paper that'll print a book like this has no principle.

HOVSTAD: Why do you jump to such extremes? You're just like . . .

PETRA: Like what?

HOVSTAD: I simply mean that . . .

PETRA, *moving away from him:* Like my father, you mean. You really have no use for him, do you?

Act Two

HOVSTAD: Now wait a minute!

PETRA: What's behind this? Are you just trying to hold my hand or something?

HOVSTAD: I happen to agree with your father, and that's why I'm printing his stuff.

PETRA: You're trying to put something over, I think. Why are you in this?

HOVSTAD: Who're you accusing? Billing gave you that book, not me!

PETRA: But you don't mind printing it, do you? What are you trying to do with my father? You have no principles—what are you up to here?

Aslaksen hurriedly enters from the printing shop, Stockmann's manuscript in his hand.

ASLAKSEN: My God! Hovstad! *He sees Petra.* Miss Stockmann.

PETRA, *looking at Hovstad:* I don't think I've been so frightened in my life. *She goes out.*

HOVSTAD, *starting after her:* Please, vou mustn't think I—

ASLAKSEN, *stopping him:* Where are vou going? The Mayor's out there.

HOVSTAD: The Mayor!

ASLAKSEN: He wants to speak to you. He came in the back door. He doesn't want to be seen.

HOVSTAD: What does he want? *He goes to the printing-room door, opens it, calls out with a certain edge of servility:* Come in, Your Honor!

PETER STOCKMANN, *entering:* Thank you.

Hovstad carefully closes the door.

PETER STOCKMANN, *walking around:* It's clean! I always imagined this place would look dirty. But it's clean. *Commendingly:* Very nice, Mr. Aslaksen. *He puts his hat on the desk.*

ASLAKSEN: Not at all, Your Honor—I mean to say, I always . . .

HOVSTAD: What can I do for you, Your Honor? Sit down?

PETER STOCKMANN, *sits, placing his cane on the table:* I had a very annoying thing happen today, Mr. Hovstad.

HOVSTAD: That so?

PETER STOCKMANN: It seems my brother has written some sort of—memorandum. About the springs.

HOVSTAD: You don't say.

PETER STOCKMANN, *looking at Hovstad now:* He mentioned it . . . to you?

HOVSTAD: Yes. I think he said something about it.

ASLAKSEN, *nervously starts to go out, attempting to hide the manuscript:* Will you excuse me, gentlemen . . .

PETER STOCKMANN, *pointing to the manuscript:* That's it, isn't it?

ASLAKSEN: This? I don't know, I haven't had a chance to look at it, the printer just handed it to me . . .

HOVSTAD: Isn't that the thing the printer wanted the spelling checked?

ASLAKSEN: That's it. it's only a question of spelling. I'll be right back.

PETER STOCKMANN: I'm very good at spelling. *He holds out his hand.* Maybe I can help you.

HOVSTAD: No, Your Honor, there's some Latin in it. You wouldn't know Latin, would you?

PETER STOCKMANN: Oh, yes. I used to help my brother with his Latin all the time. Let me have it.

Aslaksen gives him the manuscript. Peter Stockmann looks at the title on the first page, then glances up sarcastically at Hovstad, who avoids his eyes.

PETER STOCKMANN: You're going to print this?

HOVSTAD: I can't very well refuse a signed article. A signed article is the author's responsibility.

PETER STOCKMANN: Mr. Aslaksen, you're going to allow this?

ASLAKSEN: I'm the publisher, not the editor, Your Honor. My policy is freedom for the editor.

PETER STOCKMANN: You have a point—I can see that.

ASLAKSEN, *reaching for the manuscript:* So if you don't mind . . .

PETER STOCKMANN: Not at all. *But he holds on to the manuscript. After a pause:* This reconstruction of the springs—

ASLAKSEN: I realize, Your Honor—it does mean tremendous sacrifices for the stockholders.

PETER STOCKMANN: Don't upset yourself. The first thing a Mayor learns is that the less wealthy can always be prevailed upon to demand a spirit of sacrifice for the public good.

ASLAKSEN: I'm glad you see that.

PETER STOCKMANN: Oh, yes. Especially when it's the wealthy who are going to do the sacrificing. What you don't seem to understand, Mr. Aslaksen, is that so long as I am Mayor, any changes in those springs are going to be paid for by a municipal loan.

ASLAKSEN: A municipal—you mean you're going to tax the people for this?

PETER STOCKMANN: Exactly.

HOVSTAD: But the springs are a private corporation!

PETER STOCKMANN: The corporation built Kirsten Springs out of its own money. If the people want them changed, the people naturally must pay the bill. The corporation is in no position to put out any more money. It simply can't do it.

ASLAKSEN, *to Hovstad:* That's impossible! People will never stand for a new tax. *To the Mayor:* Is this a fact or your opinion?

PETER STOCKMANN: It happens to be a fact. Plus another fact —you'll forgive me for talking about facts in a newspaper office—but don't forget that the springs will take two years to make over. Two years without income for your small businessmen, Mr. Aslaksen, and a heavy new tax besides. And all because—*his private emotion comes to the surface; he throttles the manuscript in his hand*—because of this dream, this hallucination, that we live in a pesthole!

HOVSTAD: That's based on science.

PETER STOCKMANN, *raising the manuscript and throwing it down on the table:* This is based on vindictiveness, on his hatred of authority and nothing else. *He pounds on the manuscript.* This is the mad dream of a man who is trying to blow up our way of life! It has nothing to do with reform or science or anything else, but pure and simple destruction! And I intend to see to it that the people understand it exactly so!

ASLAKSEN, *hit by this:* My God! *To Hovstad:* Maybe . . . You sure you want to support this thing, Hovstad?

HOVSTAD, *nervously:* Frankly I'd never thought of it in quite that way. I mean . . . *To the Mayor:* When you think of it psychologically it's completely possible, of course, that the man is simply out to—I don't know what to say, Your Honor. I'd hate to hurt the town in any way. I never imagined we'd have to have a new tax.

PETER STOCKMANN: You should have imagined it because you're going to have to advocate it. Unless, of course, liberal and radical newspaper readers enjoy high taxes. But you'd know that better than I. I happen to have here a brief story of the actual facts. It proves that, with a little care, nobody need be harmed at all by the water. *He takes out a long envelope.* Of course, in time we'd have to make a few minor structural changes and we'd pay for those.

HOVSTAD: May I see that?

PETER STOCKMANN: I want you to *study* it, Mr. Hovstad, and see if you don't agree that—

BILLING, *entering quickly:* Are you expecting the Doctor?

PETER STOCKMANN, *alarmed:* He's here?

BILLING: Just coming across the street.

PETER STOCKMANN: I'd rather not run into him here. How can I . . .

BILLING: Right this way, sir, hurry up!

ASLAKSEN, *at the entrance door, peeking:* Hurry up!

PETER STOCKMANN, *going with Billing through the door at the left:* Get him out of here right away! *They exit.*

HOVSTAD: Do something, do something!

Aslaksen pokes among some papers on the table. Hovstad sits at the desk, starts to "write." Dr. Stockmann enters.

DR. STOCKMANN: Any proofs yet? *He sees they hardly turn to him.* I guess not, eh?

ASLAKSEN, *without turning:* No, you can't expect them for some time.

DR. STOCKMANN: You mind if I wait?

HOVSTAD: No sense in that, Doctor, it'll be quite a while yet.

DR. STOCKMANN, *laughing, places his hand on Hovstad's back:* Bear with me, Hovstad, I just can't wait to see it in print.

HOVSTAD: We're pretty busy, Doctor, so . . .

DR. STOCKMANN, *starting toward the door:* Don't let me hold you up. That's the way to be, busy, busy. We'll make this town shine like a jewel! *He has opened the door, now he comes back.* Just one thing. I—

HOVSTAD: Couldn't we talk some other time? We're very—

DR. STOCKMANN: Two words. Just walking down the street now, I looked at the people, in the stores, driving the wagons, and suddenly I was—well, touched, you know? By their innocence, I mean. What I'm driving at is, when this exposé breaks they're liable to start making a saint out of me or something, and I—Aslaksen, I want you to promise me that you're not going to try to get up any dinner for me or—

ASLAKSEN, *turning toward the Doctor:* Doctor, there's no use concealing—

DR. STOCKMANN: I knew it. Now look, I will simply not attend a dinner in my honor.

HOVSTAD, *getting up:* Doctor, I think it's time we—

Mrs. Stockmann enters.

MRS. STOCKMANN: I thought so. Thomas, I want you home. Now come. I want you to talk to Petra.

DR. STOCKMANN: What happened? What are you doing here?

HOVSTAD: Something wrong, Mrs. Stockmann?

MRS. STOCKMANN, *leveling a look of accusation at Hovstad:* Doctor Stockmann is the father of three children, Mr. Hovstad.

DR. STOCKMANN: Now look, dear, everybody knows that. What's the—

MRS. STOCKMANN, *restraining an outburst at her husband:* Nobody would *believe* it from the way you're dragging us into this disaster!

DR. STOCKMANN: What disaster?

MRS. STOCKMANN, *to Hovstad:* He treated you like a son, now you make a fool of him?

HOVSTAD: *I'm* not making a—

DR. STOCKMANN: Catherine! *He indicates Hovstad.* How can you accuse—

MRS. STOCKMANN, *to Hovstad:* He'll lose his job at the springs,

do you realize that? You print the article, and they'll grind
him up like a piece of flesh!

DR. STOCKMANN: Catherine, you're embarrassing me! I beg
your pardon, gentlemen . . .

MRS. STOCKMANN: Mr. Hovstad, what are you up to?

DR. STOCKMANN: I won't have you jumping at Hovstad, Catherine!

MRS. STOCKMANN: I want you home! This man is not your
friend!

DR. STOCKMANN: He is my friend! Any man who shares my
risk is my friend! You simply don't understand that as soon as
this breaks everybody in this town is going to come out in
the streets and drive that gang of— *He picks up the Mayor's
cane from the table, notices what it is, and stops. He looks
from it to Hovstad and Aslaksen.* What's this? *They don't re-
ply. Now he notices the hat on the desk and picks it up with
the tip of the cane. He looks at them again. He is angry, in-
credulous.* What the hell is he doing here?

ASLAKSEN: All right, Doctor, now let's be calm and—

DR. STOCKMANN, *starting to move:* Where is he? What'd he do,
talk you out of it? Hovstad! *Hovstad remains immobile.* He
won't get away with it! Where'd you hide him? *He opens the
door at the left.*

ASLAKSEN: Be careful, Doctor!

*Peter Stockmann enters with Billing through the door Dr.
Stockmann opened. Peter Stockmann tries to hide his embar-
rassment.*

DR. STOCKMANN: Well, Peter, poisoning the water was not

78

enough! You're working on the press now, eh? *He crosses to the entrance door.*

PETER STOCKMANN: My hat, please. And my stick. *Dr. Stockmann puts on the Mayor's hat.* Now what's *this* nonsense! Take that off, that's official insignia!

DR. STOCKMANN: I just wanted you to realize, Peter—*he takes off the hat and looks at it*—that anyone may wear this hat in a democracy, and that a free citizen is not afraid to touch it. *He hands him the hat.* And as for the baton of command, Your Honor, it can pass from hand to hand. *He hands the cane to Peter Stockmann.* So don't gloat yet. The people haven't spoken. *He turns to Hovstad and Aslaksen.* And I have the people because I have the truth, my friends!

ASLAKSEN: Doctor, we're not scientists. We can't judge whether your article is really true.

DR. STOCKMANN: Then print it under my name. Let *me* defend it!

HOVSTAD: I'm not printing it. I'm not going to sacrifice this newspaper. When the whole story gets out the public is not going to stand for any changes in the springs.

ASLAKSEN: His Honor just told us, Doctor—you see, there will have to be a new tax—

DR. STOCKMANN: Ahhhhh! Yes. I see. That's why you're not scientists suddenly and can't decide if I'm telling the truth. Well. So!

HOVSTAD: Don't take that attitude. The point is—

DR. STOCKMANN: The point, the point, oh, the point is going to fly through this town like an arrow, and I am going to fire it! *To Aslaksen:* Will you print this article as a pamphlet? I'll pay for it.

ASLAKSEN: I'm not going to ruin this paper and this town. Doctor, for the sake of your family—

MRS. STOCKMANN: You can leave his family out of this, Mr. Aslaksen. God help me, I think you people are horrible!

DR. STOCKMANN: My article, if you don't mind.

ASLAKSEN, *giving it to him:* Doctor, you won't get it printed in this town.

PETER STOCKMANN: Can't you forget it? *He indicates Hovstad and Aslaksen.* Can't you see now that everybody—

DR. STOCKMANN: Your Honor, I can't forget it, and you will never forget it as long as you live. I am going to call a mass meeting, and I—

PETER STOCKMANN: And who is going to rent you a hall?

DR. STOCKMANN: Then I will take a drum and go from street to street, proclaiming that the springs are befouled and poison is rotting the body politic! *He starts for the door.*

PETER STOCKMANN: And I believe you really are that mad!

DR. STOCKMANN: Mad? Oh, my brother, you haven't even heard me raise my voice yet. Catherine? *He holds out his hand, she gives him her elbow. They go stiffly out.*

Peter Stockmann looks regretfully toward the exit, then takes out his manuscript and hands it to Hovstad, who in turn gives it to Billing, who hands it to Aslaksen, who takes it and exits. Peter Stockmann puts his hat on and moves toward the door. Blackout.

The Curtain Falls.

Act Two: Scene 2

A room in Captain Horster's house. The room is bare, as though unused for a long time. A large doorway is at the left, two shuttered windows at the back, and another door at the right. Upstage right, packing cases have been set together, forming a platform, on which are a chair and a small table. There are two chairs next to the platform at the right. One chair stands downstage left.

The room is angled, thus making possible the illusion of a large crowd off in the wing to the left. The platform faces the audience at an angle, thus giving the speakers the chance to speak straight out front and creating the illusion of a large crowd by addressing "people" in the audience.

As the curtain rises the room is empty. Captain Horster enters, carrying a pitcher of water, a glass, and a bell. He is putting these on the table when Billing enters. A crowd is heard talking outside in the street.

BILLING: Captain Horster?

HORSTER, turning: Oh, come in. I don't have enough chairs for a lot of people so I decided not to have chairs at all.

BILLING: My name is Billing. Don't you remember, at the Doctor's house?

HORSTER, a little coldly: Oh, yes, sure. I've been so busy I didn't recognize you. *He goes to a window and looks out.* Why don't those people come inside?

BILLING: I don't know, I guess they're waiting for the Mayor or somebody important so they can be sure it's respectable in here. I wanted to ask you a question before it begins, Captain. Why are you lending your house for this? I never heard of you connected with anything political.

HORSTER, *standing still:* I'll answer that. I travel most of the year and—did you ever travel?

BILLING: Not abroad, no.

HORSTER: Well, I've been in a lot of places where people aren't allowed to say unpopular things. Did you know that?

BILLING: Sure, I've read about it.

HORSTER, *simply:* Well, I don't like it. *He starts to go out.*

BILLING: One more question. What's your opinion about the Doctor's proposition to rebuild the springs?

HORSTER, *turning, thinks, then:* Don't understand a thing about it.

Three citizens enter.

HORSTER: Come in, come in. I don't have enough chairs so you'll just have to stand. *He goes out.*

FIRST CITIZEN: Try the horn.

SECOND CITIZEN: No, let him start to talk first.

THIRD CITIZEN, *a big beef of a man, takes out a horn:* Wait'll they hear this! I could blow your mustache off with this!

Horster returns. He sees the horn and stops abruptly.

HORSTER: I don't want any roughhouse, you hear me?

Mrs. Stockmann and Petra enter.

HORSTER: Come in. I've got chairs just for you.

MRS. STOCKMANN, *nervously:* There's quite a crowd on the sidewalk. Why don't they come in?

HORSTER: I suppose they're waiting for the Mayor.

PETRA: Are all those people on his side?

HORSTER: Who knows? People are bashful, and it's so unusual to come to a meeting like this, I suppose they—

BILLING, *going over to this group:* Good evening, ladies. *They simply look at him.* I don't blame you for not speaking. I just wanted to say I don't think this is going to be a place for ladies tonight.

MRS. STOCKMANN: I don't remember asking your advice, Mr. Billing.

BILLING: I'm not as bad as you think, Mrs. Stockmann.

MRS. STOCKMANN: Then why did you print the Mayor's statement and not a word about my husband's report? Nobody's had a chance to find out what he really stands for. Why, everybody on the street there is against him already!

BILLING: If we printed his report it only would have hurt your husband.

MRS. STOCKMANN: Mr. Billing, I've never said this to anyone in my life, but I think you're a liar.

Suddenly the third citizen lets out a blast on his horn. The women jump, Billing and Horster turn around quickly.

HORSTER: You do that once more and I'll throw you out of here!

Peter Stockmann enters. Behind him comes the crowd. He pretends to be unconnected with them. He goes straight to Mrs. Stockmann, bows.

PETER STOCKMANN: Catherine? Petra?

PETRA: Good evening.

PETER STOCKMANN: Why so coldly? He wanted a meeting and he's got it. *To Horster:* Isn't he here?

HORSTER: The Doctor is going around town to be sure there's a good attendance.

PETER STOCKMANN: Fair enough. By the way, Petra, did you paint that poster? The one somebody stuck on the Town Hall?

PETRA: If you can call it painting, yes.

PETER STOCKMANN: You know I could arrest you? It's against the law to deface the Town Hall.

PETRA: Well, here I am. *She holds out her hands for the hand-cuffs.*

MRS. STOCKMANN, *taking it seriously:* If you arrest her, Peter, I'll never speak to you!

PETER STOCKMANN, *laughing:* Catherine, you have no sense of humor!

He crosses and sits down at the left. They sit right. A drunk comes out of the crowd.

DRUNK: Say, Billy, who's runnin'? Who's the candidate?

HORSTER: You're drunk, Mister, now get out of here!

DRUNK: There's no law says a man who's drunk can't vote!

HORSTER, *pushing the drunk toward the door as the crowd laughs:* Get out of here! Get out!

DRUNK: I wanna vote! I got a right to vote!

Aslaksen enters hurriedly, sees Peter Stockmann, and rushes to him.

ASLAKSEN: Your Honor . . . *He points to the door.* He's . . .

DR. STOCKMANN, *offstage:* Right this way, gentlemen! In you go, come on, fellows!

Hovstad enters, glances at Peter Stockmann and Aslaksen, then at Dr. Stockmann and another crowd behind him, who enter.

DR. STOCKMANN: Sorry, no chairs, gentlemen, but we couldn't get a hall, y'know, so just relax. It won't take long anyway. *He goes to the platform, sees Peter Stockmann.* Glad you're here, Peter!

PETER STOCKMANN: Wouldn't miss it for the world.

DR. STOCKMANN: How do you feel, Catherine?

MRS. STOCKMANN, *nervously:* Just promise me, don't lose your temper . . .

HORSTER, *seeing the drunk pop in through the door:* Did I tell you to get out of here!

DRUNK: Look, if you ain't votin', what the hell's going on here? *Horster starts after him.* Don't push!

PETER STOCKMANN, *to the drunk:* I order you to get out of here and stay out!

DRUNK: I don't like the tone of your voice! And if you don't watch your step I'm gonna tell the Mayor right now, and he'll throw yiz all in the jug! *To all:* What're you, a revolution here?

The crowd bursts out laughing; the drunk laughs with them, and they push him out. Dr. Stockmann mounts the platform.

DR. STOCKMANN, *quieting the crowd:* All right, gentlemen, we might as well begin. Quiet down, please. *He clears his throat.* The issue is very simple—

ASLAKSEN: We haven't elected a chairman, Doctor.

DR. STOCKMANN: I'm sorry, Mr. Aslaksen, this isn't a meeting. I advertised a lecture and I—

A CITIZEN: I came to a meeting, Doctor. There's got to be some kind of control here.

DR. STOCKMANN: What do you mean, control? What is there to control?

SECOND CITIZEN: Sure, let him speak, this is no meeting!

THIRD CITIZEN: Your Honor, why don't you take charge of this—

DR. STOCKMANN: Just a minute now!

THIRD CITIZEN: Somebody responsible has got to take charge. There's a big difference of opinion here—

DR. STOCKMANN: What makes·you so sure? You don't even know yet what I'm going to say.

THIRD CITIZEN: I've got a pretty good idea what you're going to say, and I don't like it! If a man doesn't like it here, let him go where it suits him better. We don't want any trouble-makers here!

There is assent from much of the crowd. Dr. Stockmann looks at them with new surprise.

DR. STOCKMANN: Now look, friend, you don't know anything about me—

FOURTH CITIZEN: We know plenty about you, Stockmann!

DR. STOCKMANN: From what? From the newspapers? How do you know I don't like this town? *He picks up his manuscript.* I'm here to save the life of this town!

PETER STOCKMANN, *quickly:* Now just a minute, Doctor, I think the democratic thing to do is to elect a chairman.

FIFTH CITIZEN: I nominate the Mayor!

Seconds are heard.

PETER STOCKMANN: No, no, no! That wouldn't be fair. We want a neutral person. I suggest Mr. Aslaksen—

SECOND CITIZEN: I came to a lecture, I didn't—

THIRD CITIZEN, *to second citizen:* What're you afraid of, a fair fight? *To the Mayor:* Second Mr. Aslaksen!

The crowd assents.

DR. STOCKMANN: All right, if that's your pleasure. I just want to remind you that the reason I called this meeting was that I have a very important message for you people and I couldn't get it into the press, and nobody would rent me a hall. *To Peter Stockmann:* I just hope I'll be given time to speak here. Mr. Aslaksen?

As Aslaksen mounts the platform and Dr. Stockmann steps down, Kiil enters, looks shrewdly around.

ASLAKSEN: I just have one word before we start. Whatever is

said tonight, please remember, the highest civic virtue is moderation. *He can't help turning to Dr. Stockmann, then back to the crowd.* Now if anybody wants to speak—

The drunk enters suddenly.

DRUNK, *pointing at Aslaksen:* I heard that! Since when you allowed to electioneer at the poles? *Citizens push him toward the door amid laughter.* I'm gonna report this to the Mayor, goddammit! *They push him out and close the door.*

ASLAKSEN: Quiet, please, quiet. Does anybody want the floor?

Dr. Stockmann starts to come forward, raising his hand, but Peter Stockmann also has his hand raised.

PETER STOCKMANN: Mr. Chairman!

ASLAKSEN, *quickly recognizing Peter Stockmann:* His Honor the Mayor will address the meeting.

Dr. Stockmann stops, looks at Peter Stockmann, and, suppressing a remark, returns to his place. The Mayor mounts the platform.

PETER STOCKMANN: Gentlemen, there's no reason to take very long to settle this tonight and return to our ordinary, calm, and peaceful life. Here's the issue: Doctor Stockmann, my brother—and believe me, it is not easy to say this—has decided to destroy Kirsten Springs, our Health Institute—

DR. STOCKMANN: Peter!

ASLAKSEN, *ringing his bell:* Let the Mayor continue, please. There mustn't be any interruptions.

PETER STOCKMANN: He has a long and very involved way of going about it, but that's the brunt of it, believe me.

THIRD CITIZEN: Then what're we wasting time for? Run him out of town!

Others join in the cry.

PETER STOCKMANN: Now wait a minute. I want no violence here. I want you to understand his motives. He is a man, always has been, who is never happy unless he is badgering authority, ridiculing authority, destroying authority. He wants to attack the springs so he can prove that the administration blundered in the construction.

DR. STOCKMANN, *to Aslaksen:* May I speak? I—

ASLAKSEN: The Mayor's not finished.

PETER STOCKMANN: Thank you. Now there are a number of people here who seem to feel that the Doctor has a right to say anything he pleases. After all, we are a democratic country. Now, God knows, in ordinary times I'd agree a hundred per cent with anybody's right to say anything. But these are not ordinary times. Nations have crises, and so do towns. There are ruins of nations, and there are ruins of towns all over the world, and they were wrecked by people who, in the guise of reform, and pleading for justice, and so on, broke down all authority and left only revolution and chaos.

DR. STOCKMANN: What the hell are you talking about!

ASLAKSEN: I'll have to insist, Doctor—

DR. STOCKMANN: I called a lecture! I didn't invite him to attack me. He's got the press and every hall in town to attack me, and I've got nothing but this room tonight!

ASLAKSEN: I don't think you're making a very good impression, Doctor.

Assenting laughter and catcalls. Again Dr. Stockmann is taken aback by this reaction.

ASLAKSEN: Please continue, Your Honor.

PETER STOCKMANN: Now this is our crisis. We know what this town was without our Institute. We could barely afford to keep the streets in condition. It was a dead, third-rate hamlet. Today we're just on the verge of becoming internationally known as a resort. I predict that within five years the income of every man in this room will be immensely greater. I predict that our schools will be bigger and better. And in time this town will be crowded with fine carriages; great homes will be built here; first-class stores will open all along Main Street. I predict that if we are not defamed and maliciously attacked we will someday be one of the richest and most beautiful resort towns in the world. There are your choices. Now all you've got to do is ask yourselves a simple question: Has any one of us the right, the "democratic right," as they like to call it, to pick at minor flaws in the springs, to exaggerate the most picayune faults? *Cries of No, No!* And to attempt to publish these defamations for the whole world to see? We live or die on what the outside world thinks of us. I believe there is a line that must be drawn, and if a man decides to cross that line, we the people must finally take him by the collar and declare, "You cannot say that!"

There is an uproar of assent. Aslaksen rings the bell.

PETER STOCKMANN, *continuing:* All right then. I think we all understand each other. Mr. Aslaksen, I move that Doctor Stockmann be prohibited from reading his report at this meeting! *He goes back to his chair, which meanwhile Kiil has occupied.*

Aslaksen rings the bell to quiet the enthusiasm. Dr. Stockmann is jumping to get up on the platform, the report in his hand.

ASLAKSEN: Quiet, please. Please now. I think we can proceed to the vote.

DR. STOCKMANN: Well, aren't you going to let me speak at all?

ASLAKSEN: Doctor, we are just about to vote on that question.

DR. STOCKMANN: But damn it, man, I've got a right to—

PETRA, *standing up:* Point of order, Father!

DR. STOCKMANN, *picking up the cue:* Yes, point of order!

ASLAKSEN, *turning to him now:* Yes, Doctor.

Dr. Stockmann, at a loss, turns to Petra for further instructions.

PETRA: You want to discuss the motion.

DR. STOCKMANN: That's right, damn it, I want to discuss the motion!

ASLAKSEN: Ah . . . *He glances at Peter Stockmann.* All right, go ahead.

DR. STOCKMANN, *to the crowd:* Now, listen. *He points at Peter Stockmann.* He talks and he talks and he talks, but not a word about the facts! *He holds up the manuscript.*

THIRD CITIZEN: We don't want to hear any more about the water!

FOURTH CITIZEN: You're just trying to blow up everything!

DR. STOCKMANN: Well, judge for yourselves, let me read—

Cries of No, No, No! The man with the horn blows it. Aslak-
sen rings the bell. Dr. Stockmann is utterly shaken. Aston-
ished, he looks at the maddened faces. He lowers the hand
holding the manuscript and steps back, defeated.

ASLAKSEN: Please, please now, quiet. We can't have this uproar! *Quiet returns.* I think, Doctor, that the majority wants
to take the vote before you start to speak. If they so will, you
can speak. Otherwise, majority rules. You won't deny that.

DR. STOCKMANN, *turns, tosses the manuscript on the floor,*
turns back to Aslaksen: Don't bother voting. I understand
everything now. Can I have a few minutes—

PETER STOCKMANN: Mr. Chairman!

DR. STOCKMANN, *to his brother:* I won't mention the Institute.
I have a new discovery that's a thousand times more important
than all the Institutes in the world. *To Aslaksen:* May I have
the platform.

ASLAKSEN, *to the crowd:* I don't see how we can deny him
that, as long as he confines himself to—

DR. STOCKMANN: The springs are not the subject. *He mounts*
the platform, looks at the crowd. Before I go into my subject
I want to congratulate the liberals and radicals among us,
like Mr. Hovstad—

HOVSTAD: What do you mean, radical! Where's your evidence
to call me a radical!

DR. STOCKMANN: You've got me there. There isn't any evidence. I guess there never really was. I just wanted to congratulate you on your self-control tonight—you who have
fought in every parlor for the principle of free speech these
many years.

HOVSTAD: I believe in democracy. When my readers are over-whelmingly against something, I'm not going to impose my will on the majority.

DR. STOCKMANN: You have begun my remarks, Mr. Hovstad. *He turns to the crowd.* Gentlemen, Mrs. Stockmann, Miss Stockma.. Tonight I was struck by a sudden flash of light, a discovery s.. d to none. But before I tell it to you—a little story. I put in a d many years in the north of our country. Up there the rule.. the world are the great seal and the gigantic squadrons o. k. Man lives on ice, huddled to-gether in little piles of es. His whole life consists of grubbing for food. Nothing e. He can barely speak his own language. And it came to m. e day that it was roman-tic and sentimental for a man of my cation to be tending these people. They had not yet reached stage where they needed a doctor. If the truth were to be a veterinary would be more in order.

BILLING: Is that the way you refer to decent har.. rking people!

DR. STOCKMANN: I expected that, my friend, but don't think you can fog up my brain with that magic word—the People! Not any more! Just because there is a mass of organisms with the human shape, they do not automatically become a People. That honor has to be earned! Nor does one automatically become a Man by having human shape, and living in a house, and feeding one's face—and agreeing with one's neighbors. That name *also* has to be earned. Now, when I came to my conclusions about the springs—

PETER STOCKMANN: You have no right to—

DR. STOCKMANN: That's a picayune thing, to catch me on a word, Peter. I am not going into the springs. *To the crowd:*

When I became convinced of my theory about the water, the authorities moved in at once, and I said to myself, I will fight them to the death, because—

THIRD CITIZEN: What're you trying to do, make a revolution here? He's a revolutionist!

DR. STOCKMANN: Let me finish. I thought to myself: The majority, I have the majority! And let me tell you, friends, it was a grand feeling. Because that's the reason I came back to this place of my birth. I wanted to give my education to this town. I loved it so, I spent months without pay or encouragement and dreamed up the whole project of the springs. And why? Not as my brother says, so that fine carriages could crowd our streets, but so that we might cure the sick, so that we might meet people from all over the world and learn from them, and become broader and more civilized. In other words, more like Men, more like A People.

A CITIZEN: You don't like anything about this town, do you?

ANOTHER CITIZEN: Admit it, you're a revolutionist, aren't you? Admit it!

DR. STOCKMANN: I don't admit it! I proclaim it now! I am a revolutionist! I am in revolt against the age-old lie that the majority is always right!

HOVSTAD: He's an aristocrat all of a sudden!

DR. STOCKMANN: And more! I tell you now that the majority is always wrong, and in this way!

PETER STOCKMANN: Have you lost your mind! Stop talking before—

DR. STOCKMANN: Was the majority right when they stood by while Jesus was crucified? *Silence.* Was the majority right when they refused to believe that the earth moved around the sun and let Galileo be driven to his knees like a dog? It takes fifty years for the majority to be right. The majority is never right until it *does* right.

HOVSTAD: I want to state right now, that although I've been this man's friend, and I've eaten at his table many times, I now cut myself off from him absolutely.

DR. STOCKMANN: Answer me this! Please, one more moment! A platoon of soldiers is walking down a road toward the enemy. Every one of them is convinced he is on the right road, the safe road. But two miles ahead stands one lonely man, the outpost. He sees that this road is dangerous, that his comrades are walking into a trap. He runs back, he finds the platoon. Isn't it clear that this man must have the right to warn the majority, to argue with the majority, to fight with the majority if he believes he has the truth? Before many can know something, *one* must know it! *His passion has silenced the crowd.* It's always the same. Rights are sacred until it hurts for somebody to use them. I beg you now—I realize the cost is great, the inconvenience is great, the risk is great that other towns will get the jump on us while we're rebuilding—

PETER STOCKMANN: Aslaksen, he's not allowed to—

DR. STOCKMANN: Let me prove it to you! The water is poisoned!

THIRD CITIZEN, *steps up on the platform, waves his fist in Dr. Stockmann's face:* One more word about poison and I'm gonna take you outside!

The crowd is roaring; some try to charge the platform. The horn is blowing. Aslaksen rings his bell. Peter Stockmann steps forward, raising his hands. Kiil quietly exits.

PETER STOCKMANN: That's enough. Now stop it! Quiet! There is not going to be any violence here! *There is silence. He turns to Dr. Stockmann.* Doctor, come down and give Mr. Aslaksen the platform.

DR. STOCKMANN, *staring down at the crowd with new eyes:* I'm not through yet.

PETER STOCKMANN: Come down or I will not be responsible for what happens.

MRS. STOCKMANN: I'd like to go home. Come on, Tom.

PETER STOCKMANN: I move the chairman order the speaker to leave the platform.

VOICES: Sit down! Get off that platform!

DR. STOCKMANN: All right. Then I'll take this to out-of-town newspapers until the whole country is warned!

PETER STOCKMANN: You wouldn't dare!

HOVSTAD: You're trying to ruin this town—that's all; trying to ruin it.

DR. STOCKMANN: You're trying to build a town on a morality so rotten that it will infect the country and the world! If the only way you can prosper is this murder of freedom and truth, then I say with all my heart, "Let it be destroyed! Let the people perish!"

He leaves the platform.

FIRST CITIZEN, *to the Mayor:* Arrest him! Arrest him!

SECOND CITIZEN: He's a traitor!

Cries of "Enemy! Traitor! Revolution!"

ASLAKSEN, *ringing for quiet:* I would like to submit the following resolution: The people assembled here tonight, decent and patriotic citizens, in defense of their town and their country, declare that Doctor Stockmann, medical officer of Kirsten Springs, is an enemy of the people and of his community.

An uproar of assent starts.

MRS. STOCKMANN, *getting up:* That's not true! He loves this town!

DR. STOCKMANN: You damned fools, you fools!

The Doctor and his family are all standing together, at the right, in a close group.

ASLAKSEN, *shouting over the din:* Is there anyone against this motion! Anyone against!

HORSTER, *raising his hand:* I am.

ASLAKSEN: One? *He looks around.*

DRUNK, *who has returned, raising his hand:* Me too! You can't do without a doctor! Anybody'll . . . tell you . . .

ASLAKSEN: Anyone else? With all votes against two, this assembly formally declares Doctor Thomas Stockmann to be the people's enemy. In the future, all dealings with him by decent, patriotic citizens will be on that basis. The meeting is adjourned.

Shouts and applause. People start leaving. Dr. Stockmann goes over to Horster.

DR. STOCKMANN: Captain, do you have room for us on your ship to America?

HORSTER: Any time you say, Doctor.

DR. STOCKMANN: Catherine? Petra?

The three start for the door, but a gantlet has formed, dangerous and silent, except for

THIRD CITIZEN: You'd better get aboard soon, Doctor!

MRS. STOCKMANN: Let's go out the back door.

HORSTER: Right this way.

DR. STOCKMANN: No, no. No back doors. *To the crowd:* I don't want to mislead anybody—the enemy of the people is not finished in this town—not quite yet. And if anybody thinks—

The horn blasts, cutting him off. The crowd starts yelling hysterically: "Enemy! Traitor! Throw him in the river! Come on, throw him in the river! Enemy! Enemy! Enemy!" The Stockmanns, erect, move out through the crowd, with Horster. Some of the crowd follow them out, yelling.

Downstage, watching, are Peter Stockmann, Billing, Aslaksen, and Hovstad. The stage is throbbing with the chant, "Enemy, Enemy, Enemy!" as

The Curtain Falls.

Act Three

Dr. Stockmann's living room the following morning. The windows are broken. There is great disorder. As the curtain rises, Dr. Stockmann enters, a robe over shirt and trousers—it's cold in the house. He picks up a stone from the floor, lays it on the table.

DR. STOCKMANN: Catherine! Tell what's-her-name there are still some rocks to pick up in here.

MRS. STOCKMANN, *from inside:* She's not finished sweeping up the glass.

As Dr. Stockmann bends down to get at another stone under a chair a rock comes through one of the last remaining panes. He rushes to the window, looks out. Mrs. Stockmann rushes in.

MRS. STOCKMANN, *frightened:* You all right?

DR. STOCKMANN, *looking out:* A little boy. Look at him run! *He picks up the stone.* How fast the poison spreads—even to the children!

MRS. STOCKMANN, *looking out the window:* It's hard to believe this is the same town.

DR. STOCKMANN, *adding this rock to the pile on the table:* I'm going to keep these like sacred relics. I'll put them in my

99

will. I want the boys to have them in their homes to look at every day. *He shudders.* Cold in here. Why hasn't what's-her-name got the glazier here?

MRS. STOCKMANN: She's getting him . . .

DR. STOCKMANN: She's been getting him for two hours! We'll freeze to death in here.

MRS. STOCKMANN, *unwillingly:* He won't come here, Tom.

DR. STOCKMANN, *stops moving:* No! The glazier's afraid to fix my windows?

MRS. STOCKMANN: You don't realize—people don't like to be pointed out. He's got neighbors, I suppose, and— *She hears something.* Is that someone at the door, Randine?

She goes to front door. He continues picking up stones. She comes back.

MRS. STOCKMANN: Letter for you.

DR. STOCKMANN, *taking and opening it:* What's this now?

MRS. STOCKMANN, *continuing his pick-up for him:* I don't know how we're going to do any shopping with everybody ready to bite my head off and—

DR. STOCKMANN: Well, what do you know? We're evicted.

MRS. STOCKMANN: Oh, no!

DR. STOCKMANN: He hates to do it, but with public opinion what it is . . .

MRS. STOCKMANN, *frightened:* Maybe we shouldn't have let the boys go to school today.

DR. STOCKMANN: Now don't get all frazzled again.

MRS. STOCKMANN: But the landlord is such a nice man. If he's got to throw us out, the town must be ready to murder us!

DR. STOCKMANN: Just calm down, will you? We'll go to America, and the whole thing'll be like a dream.

MRS. STOCKMANN: But I don't want to go to America— *She notices his pants.* When did this get torn?

DR. STOCKMANN, *examining the tear:* Must've been last night.

MRS. STOCKMANN: Your best pants!

DR. STOCKMANN: Well, it just shows you, that's all—when a man goes out to fight for the truth he should never wear his best pants. *He calms her.* Stop worrying, will you? You'll sew them up, and in no time at all we'll be three thousand miles away.

MRS. STOCKMANN: But how do you know it'll be any different there?

DR. STOCKMANN: I don't know. It just seems to me, in a big country like that, the spirit must be bigger. Still, I suppose they must have the solid majority there too. I don't know, at least there must be more room to hide there.

MRS. STOCKMANN: Think about it more, will you? I'd hate to go half around the world and find out we're in the same place.

DR. STOCKMANN: You know, Catherine, I don't think I'm ever going to forget the face of that crowd last night.

MRS. STOCKMANN: Don't think about it.

DR. STOCKMANN: Some of them had their teeth bared, like

animals in a pack. And who leads them? Men who call themselves liberals! Radicals! *She starts looking around at the furniture, figuring.* The crowd lets out one roar, and where are they, my liberal friends? I bet if I walked down the street now not one of them would admit he ever met me! Are you listening to me?

MRS. STOCKMANN: I was just wondering what we'll ever do with this furniture if we go to America.

DR. STOCKMANN: Don't you ever listen when I talk, dear?

MRS. STOCKMANN: Why must I listen? I know you're right.

Petra enters.

MRS. STOCKMANN: Petra! Why aren't you in school?

DR. STOCKMANN: What's the matter?

PETRA, *with deep emotion, looks at Dr. Stockmann, goes up and kisses him:* I'm fired.

MRS. STOCKMANN: They wouldn't!

PETRA: As of two weeks from now. But I couldn't bear to stay there.

DR. STOCKMANN, *shocked:* Mrs. Busk fired you?

MRS. STOCKMANN: Who'd ever imagine she could do such a thing!

PETRA: It hurt her. I could see it, because we've always agreed so about things. But she didn't dare do anything else.

DR. STOCKMANN: The glazier doesn't dare fix the windows, the landlord doesn't dare let us stay on—

PETRA: The landlord!

DR. STOCKMANN: Evicted, darling! Oh, God, on the wreckage of all the civilizations in the world there ought to be a big sign: "They Didn't Dare!"

PETRA: I really can't blame her, Father. She showed me three letters she got this morning—

DR. STOCKMANN: From whom?

PETRA: They weren't signed.

DR. STOCKMANN: Oh, naturally. The big patriots with their anonymous indignation, scrawling out the darkness of their minds onto dirty little slips of paper—that's morality, and *I'm* the traitor! What did the letters say?

PETRA: Well, one of them was from somebody who said that he'd heard at the club that somebody who visits this house said that I had radical opinions about certain things.

DR. STOCKMANN: Oh, wonderful! Somebody heard that somebody heard that she heard, that he heard . . . ! Catherine, pack as soon as you can. I feel as though vermin were crawling all over me.

Horster enters.

HORSTER: Good morning.

DR. STOCKMANN: Captain! You're just the man I want to see.

HORSTER: I thought I'd see how you all were.

MRS. STOCKMANN: That's awfully nice of you, Captain, and I want to thank you for seeing us through the crowd last night.

PETRA: Did you get home all right? We hated to leave you alone with that mob.

HORSTER: Oh, nothing to it. In a storm there's just one thing to remember: it will pass.

DR. STOCKMANN: Unless it kills you.

HORSTER: You mustn't let yourself get too bitter.

DR. STOCKMANN: I'm trying, I'm trying. But I don't guarantee how I'll feel when I try to walk down the street with "Traitor" branded on my forehead.

MRS. STOCKMANN: Don't think about it.

HORSTER: Ah, what's a word?

DR. STOCKMANN: A word can be like a needle sticking in your heart, Captain. It can dig and corrode like an acid, until you become what they want you to be—really an enemy of the people.

HORSTER: You mustn't ever let that happen, Doctor.

DR. STOCKMANN: Frankly, I don't give a damn any more. Let summer come, let an epidemic break out, then they'll know whom they drove into exile. When are you sailing?

PETRA: You really decided to go, Father?

DR. STOCKMANN: Absolutely. When do you sail, Captain?

HORSTER: That's really what I came to talk to you about.

DR. STOCKMANN: Why? Something happen to the ship?

MRS. STOCKMANN, *happily, to Dr. Stockmann:* You see! We can't go!

HORSTER: No, the ship will sail. But I won't be aboard.

DR. STOCKMANN: No!

PETRA: You fired too? 'Cause I was this morning.

MRS. STOCKMANN: Oh, Captain, you shouldn't have given us your house.

HORSTER: Oh, I'll get another ship. It's just that the owner, Mr. Vik, happens to belong to the same party as the Mayor, and I suppose when you belong to a party, and the party takes a certain position . . . Because Mr. Vik himself is a very decent man.

DR. STOCKMANN: Oh, they're all decent men!

HORSTER: No, really, he's not like the others.

DR. STOCKMANN: He doesn't have to be. A party is like a sausage grinder: it mashes up clearheads, longheads, fatheads, blockheads—and what comes out? Meatheads!

There is a knock on the hall door. Petra goes to answer.

MRS. STOCKMANN: Maybe that's the glazier!

DR. STOCKMANN: Imagine, Captain! *He points to the window.* Refused to come all morning!

Peter Stockmann enters, his hat in his hand. Silence.

PETER STOCKMANN: If you're busy . . .

DR. STOCKMANN: Just picking up broken glass. Come in, Peter. What can I do for you this fine, brisk morning? *He demonstratively pulls his robe tighter around his throat.*

MRS. STOCKMANN: Come inside, won't you, Captain?

HORSTER: Yes, I'd like to finish our talk, Doctor.

DR. STOCKMANN: Be with you in a minute, Captain.

Horster follows Petra and Catherine out through the dining-

room doorway. Peter Stockmann says nothing, looking at the damage.

DR. STOCKMANN: Keep your hat on if you like, it's a little drafty in here today.

PETER STOCKMANN: Thanks, I believe I will. *He puts his hat on.* I think I caught cold last night—that house was freezing.

DR. STOCKMANN: I thought it was kind of warm—suffocating, as a matter of fact. What do you want?

PETER STOCKMANN: May I sit down? *He indicates a chair near the window.*

DR. STOCKMANN: Not there. A piece of the solid majority is liable to open your skull. Here.

They sit on the couch. Peter Stockmann takes out a large envelope.

DR. STOCKMANN: Now don't tell me.

PETER STOCKMANN: Yes. *He hands the Doctor the envelope.*

DR. STOCKMANN: I'm fired.

PETER STOCKMANN: The Board met this morning. There was nothing else to do, considering the state of public opinion.

DR. STOCKMANN, *after a pause:* You look scared, Peter.

PETER STOCKMANN: I—I haven't completely forgotten that you're still my brother.

DR. STOCKMANN: I doubt that.

PETER STOCKMANN: You have no practice left in this town, Thomas.

DR. STOCKMANN: Oh, people always need a doctor.

PETER STOCKMANN: A petition is going from house to house. Everybody is signing it. A pledge not to call you any more. I don't think a single family will dare refuse to sign it.

DR. STOCKMANN: You started that, didn't you?

PETER STOCKMANN: No. As a matter of fact, I think it's all gone a little too far. I never wanted to see you ruined, Thomas. This will ruin you.

DR. STOCKMANN: No, it won't.

PETER STOCKMANN: For once in your life, will you act like a responsible man?

DR. STOCKMANN: Why don't you say it, Peter? You're afraid I'm going out of town to start publishing about the springs, aren't you?

PETER STOCKMANN: I don't deny that. Thomas, if you really have the good of the town at heart, you can accomplish everything without damaging anybody, including yourself.

DR. STOCKMANN: What's this now?

PETER STOCKMANN: Let me have a signed statement saying that in your zeal to help the town you went overboard and exaggerated. Put it any way you like, just so you calm anybody who might feel nervous about the water. If you'll give me that, you've got your job. And I give you my word, you can gradually make all the improvements you feel are necessary. Now, that gives you what you want . . .

DR. STOCKMANN: You're nervous, Peter.

PETER STOCKMANN, *nervously:* I am not nervous!

DR. STOCKMANN: You expect me to remain in charge while people are being poisoned? *He gets up.*

PETER STOCKMANN: In time you can make your changes.

DR. STOCKMANN: When, five years, ten years? You know your trouble, Peter? You just don't grasp—even now—that there are certain men you can't buy.

PETER STOCKMANN: I'm quite capable of understanding that. But you don't happen to be one of those men.

DR. STOCKMANN, *after a slight pause:* What do you mean by that now?

PETER STOCKMANN: You know damned well what I mean by that. Morten Kiil is what I mean by that.

DR. STOCKMANN: Morten Kiil?

PETER STOCKMANN: Your father-in-law, Morten Kiil.

DR. STOCKMANN: I swear, Peter, one of us is out of his mind! What are you talking about?

PETER STOCKMANN: Now don't try to charm me with that professional innocence!

DR. STOCKMANN: What are you talking about?

PETER STOCKMANN: You don't know that your father-in-law has been running around all morning buying up stock in Kirsten Springs?

DR. STOCKMANN, *perplexed:* Buying up stock?

PETER STOCKMANN: Buying up stock, every share he can lay his hands on!

DR. STOCKMANN: Well, I don't understand, Peter. What's that got to do with—

PETER STOCKMANN, *walking around agitatedly:* Oh, come now, come now, come now!

DR. STOCKMANN: I hate you when you do that! Don't just walk around gabbling "Come now, come now!" What the hell are you talking about?

PETER STOCKMANN: Very well, if you insist on being dense. A man wages a relentless campaign to destroy confidence in a corporation. He even goes so far as to call a mass meeting against it. The very next morning, when people are still in a state of shock about it all, his father-in-law runs all over town, picking up shares at half their value.

DR. STOCKMANN, *realizing, turns away:* My God!

PETER STOCKMANN: And you have the nerve to speak to me about principles!

DR. STOCKMANN: You mean you actually believe that I . . . ?

PETER STOCKMANN: I'm not interested in psychology! I believe what I see! And what I see is nothing but a man doing a dirty, filthy job for Morten Kiil. And let me tell you—by tonight every man in this town'll see the same thing!

DR. STOCKMANN: Peter, you, you . . .

PETER STOCKMANN: Now go to your desk and write me a statement denying everything you've been saying, or . . .

DR. STOCKMANN: Peter, you're a low creature!

PETER STOCKMANN: All right then, you'd better get this one straight, Thomas. If you're figuring on opening another attack from out of town, keep this in mind: the morning it's published I'll send out a subpoena for you and begin a prosecution for conspiracy. I've been trying to make you respectable all my life; now if you want to make the big jump there'll be nobody there to hold you back. Now do we understand each other?

DR. STOCKMANN: Oh, we do, Peter! *Peter Stockmann starts for the door.* Get the girl—what the hell is her name—scrub the floors, wash down the walls, a pestilence has been here!

Kiil enters. Peter Stockmann almost runs into him. Peter turns to his brother.

PETER STOCKMANN, *pointing to Kiil:* Ha! *He turns and goes out.*

Kiil, humming quietly, goes to a chair.

DR. STOCKMANN: Morten! What have you done? What's the matter with you? Do you realize what this makes me look like?

Kiil has started taking some papers out of his pocket. Dr. Stockmann breaks off on seeing them. Kiil places them on the table.

DR. STOCKMANN: Is that—them?

KIIL: That's them, yes. Kirsten Springs shares. And very easy to get this morning.

DR. STOCKMANN: Morten, don't play with me—what is this all about?

KIIL: What are you so nervous about? Can't a man buy some stock without . . . ?

DR. STOCKMANN: I want an explanation, Morten.

KIIL, *nodding:* Thomas, they hated you last night—

DR. STOCKMANN: You don't have to tell me that.

KIIL: But they also believed you. They'd love to murder you, but they believe you. *Slight pause.* The way they say it, the pollution is coming down the river from Windmill Valley.

DR. STOCKMANN: That's exactly where it's coming from.

KIIL: Yes. And that's exactly where my tannery is.

Pause. Dr. Stockmann sits down slowly.

DR. STOCKMANN: Well, Morten, I never made a secret to you that the pollution was tannery waste.

KIIL: I'm not blaming you. It's my fault. I didn't take you seriously. But it's very serious now. Thomas, I got that tannery from my father; he got it from his father; and his father got it from my great-grandfather. I do not intend to allow my family's name to stand for the three generations of murdering angels who poisoned this town.

DR. STOCKMANN: I've waited a long time for this talk, Morten. I don't think you can stop that from happening.

KIIL: No, but you can.

DR. STOCKMANN: I?

KIIL, *nudging the shares:* I've bought these shares because—

DR. STOCKMANN: Morten, you've thrown your money away. The springs are doomed.

KIIL: I never throw my money away, Thomas. These were bought with your money.

DR. STOCKMANN: My money? What . . . ?

KIIL: You've probably suspected that I might leave a little something for Catherine and the boys?

DR. STOCKMANN: Well, naturally, I'd hoped you'd . . .

KIIL, *touching the shares:* I decided this morning to invest that money in some stock.

DR. STOCKMANN, *slowly getting up:* You bought that junk with Catherine's money!

KIIL: People call me "badger," and that's an animal that roots out things, but it's also some kind of a pig, I understand. I've lived a clean man and I'm going to die clean. You're going to clean my name for me.

DR. STOCKMANN: Morten . . .

KIIL: Now I want to see if you really belong in a strait jacket.

DR. STOCKMANN: How could you do such a thing? What's the matter with you!

KIIL: Now don't get excited, it's very simple. If you should make another investigation of the water—

DR. STOCKMANN: I don't *need* another investigation, I—

KIIL: If you think it over and decide that you ought to change your opinion about the water—

DR. STOCKMANN: But the water is poisoned! It is poisoned!

KIIL: If you simply go on insisting the water is poisoned—*he holds up the shares*—with these in your house, then there's only one explanation for you—you're absolutely crazy. *He puts the shares down on the table again.*

DR. STOCKMANN: You're right! I'm mad! I'm insane!

KIIL, *with more force:* You're stripping the skin off your family's back! Only a madman would do a thing like that!

DR. STOCKMANN: Morten, Morten, I'm a penniless man! Why didn't you tell me before you bought this junk?

KIIL: Because you would understand it better if I told you after. *He goes up to Dr. Stockmann, holds him by the lapels.*

With terrific force, and the twinkle still in his eye: And, god-dammit, I think you do understand it now, don't you? Millions of tons of water come down that river. How do you know the day you made your tests there wasn't something unusual about the water?

DR. STOCKMANN, *not looking at Kiil:* Yes, but I . . .

KIIL: How do you know? Why couldn't those little animals have clotted up only the patch of water you souped out of the river? How do you know the rest of it wasn't pure?

DR. STOCKMANN: It's not probable. People were getting sick last summer . . .

KIIL: They were sick when they came here or they wouldn't have come!

DR. STOCKMANN, *breaking away:* Not intestinal diseases, skin diseases . . .

KIIL, *following him:* The only place anybody gets a bellyache is here! There are no carbuncles in Norway? Maybe the food was bad. Did you ever think of the food?

DR. STOCKMANN, *with the desire to agree with him:* No, I didn't look into the food . . .

KIIL: Then what makes you so sure it's the water?

DR. STOCKMANN: Because I tested the water and—

KIIL, *taking hold of him again:* Admit it! We're all alone here. You have some doubt.

DR. STOCKMANN: Well, there's always a possible . . .

KIIL: Then part of it's imaginary.

DR. STOCKMANN: Well, nothing is a hundred per cent on this earth, but—

KIIL: Then you have a perfect right to doubt the other way! You have a scientific right! And did you ever think of some disinfectant? I bet you never even thought of that.

DR. STOCKMANN: Not for a mass of water like that, you can't . . .

KIIL: Everything can be killed. That's science! Thomas, I never liked your brother either, you have a perfect right to hate him.

DR. STOCKMANN: I didn't do it because I hate my brother.

KIIL: Part of it, part of it, don't deny it! You admit there's some doubt in your mind about the water, you admit there may be ways to disinfect it, and yet you went after your brother as though these doubts didn't exist; as though the only way to cure the thing was to blow up the whole Institute! There's hatred in that, boy, don't forget it. *He points to the shares.* These can belong to you now, so be sure, be sure! Tear the hatred out of your heart, stand naked in front of yourself—*are you sure?*

DR. STOCKMANN: What right have you to gamble my family's future on the strength of my convictions?

KIIL: Aha! Then the convictions are not really that strong!

DR. STOCKMANN: I am ready to hang for my convictions! But no man has a right to make martyrs of others; my family is innocent. Sell back those shares, give her what belongs to her. I'm a penniless man!

KIIL: Nobody is going to say Morten Kiil wrecked this town.

He gathers up the shares. You retract your convictions—or these go to my charity.

DR. STOCKMANN: Everything?

KIIL: There'll be a little something for Catherine, but not much. I want my good name. It's exceedingly important to me.

DR. STOCKMANN, *bitterly:* And charity . . .

KIIL: Charity will do it, or you will do it. It's a serious thing to destroy a town.

DR. STOCKMANN: Morten, when I look at you, I swear to God I see the devil!

The door opens, and before we see who is there . . .

DR. STOCKMANN: You!

Aslaksen enters, holding up his hand defensively.

ASLAKSEN: Now don't get excited! Please!

Hovstad enters. He and Aslaksen stop short and smile on seeing Kiil.

KIIL: Too many intellectuals here: I'd better go.

ASLAKSEN, *apologetically:* Doctor, can we have five minutes of—

DR. STOCKMANN: I've got nothing to say to you.

KIIL, *going to the door:* I want an answer right away. You hear? I'm waiting. *He leaves.*

DR. STOCKMANN: All right, say it quick, what do you want?

HOVSTAD: We don't expect you to forgive our attitude at the meeting, but . . .

DR. STOCKMANN, *groping for the word:* Your attitude was prone . . . prostrated . . . prostituted!

HOVSTAD: All right, call it whatever you—

DR. STOCKMANN: I've got a lot on my mind, so get to the point. What do you want?

ASLAKSEN: Doctor, you should have told us what was in back of it all. You could have had the *Messenger* behind you all the way.

HOVSTAD: You'd have had public opinion with you now. Why didn't you tell us?

DR. STOCKMANN: Look, I'm very tired, let's not beat around the bush!

HOVSTAD, *gesturing toward the door where Kiil went out:* He's been all over town buying up stock in the springs. It's no secret any more.

DR. STOCKMANN, *after a slight pause:* Well, what about it?

HOVSTAD, *in a friendly way:* You don't want me to spell it out, do you?

DR. STOCKMANN: I certainly wish you would. I—

HOVSTAD: All right, let's lay it on the table. Aslaksen, you want to . . . ?

ASLAKSEN: No, no, go ahead.

HOVSTAD: Doctor, in the beginning we supported you. But it quickly became clear that if we kept on supporting you in the face of public hysteria—

DR. STOCKMANN: Your paper created the hysteria.

Act Three

HOVSTAD: One thing at a time, all right? *Slowly, to drive it into Dr. Stockmann's head:* We couldn't go on supporting you because, in simple language, we didn't have the money to withstand the loss in circulation. You're boycotted now? Well, the paper would have been boycotted too, if we'd stuck with you.

ASLAKSEN: You can see that, Doctor.

DR. STOCKMANN: Oh, yes. But what do you want?

HOVSTAD: *The People's Messenger* can put on such a campaign that in two months you will be hailed as a hero in this town.

ASLAKSEN: We're ready to go.

HOVSTAD: We will prove to the public that you had to buy up the stock because the management would not make the changes required for public health. In other words, you did it for absolutely scientific, public-spirited reasons. Now what do you say, Doctor?

DR. STOCKMANN: You want money from me, is that it?

ASLAKSEN: Well, now, Doctor . . .

HOVSTAD, *to Aslaksen:* No, don't walk around it. *To Dr. Stockmann:* If we started to support you again, Doctor, we'd lose circulation for a while. We'd like you—or Mr. Kiil rather—to make up the deficit. *Quickly:* Now that's open and aboveboard, and I don't see anything wrong with it. Do you?

Pause. Dr. Stockmann looks at him, then turns and walks to the windows, deep in thought.

ASLAKSEN: Remember, Doctor, you need the paper, you need it desperately.

DR. STOCKMANN, *returning:* No, there's nothing wrong with it at all. I—I'm not at all averse to cleaning up my name—although for myself it never was dirty. But I don't *enjoy* being hated, if you know what I mean.

ASLAKSEN: Exactly.

HOVSTAD: Aslaksen, will you show him the budget . . .

Aslaksen reaches into his pocket.

DR. STOCKMANN: Just a minute. There is one point. I hate to keep repeating the same thing, but the water is poisoned.

HOVSTAD: Now, Doctor . . .

DR. STOCKMANN: Just a minute. The Mayor says that he will levy a tax on everybody to pay for the reconstruction. I assume you are ready to support that tax at the same time you're supporting me.

ASLAKSEN: That tax would be extremely unpopular.

HOVSTAD: Doctor, with you back in charge of the baths, I have absolutely no fear that anything can go wrong.

DR. STOCKMANN: In other words, you will clean up my name— so that I can be in charge of the corruption.

HOVSTAD: But we can't tackle everything at once. A new tax— there'd be an uproar!

ASLAKSEN: It would ruin the paper!

DR. STOCKMANN: Then you don't intend to do anything about the water?

HOVSTAD: We have faith you won't let anyone get sick.

DR. STOCKMANN: In other words, gentlemen, you are looking for someone to blackmail into paying your printing bill.

HOVSTAD, *indignantly:* We are trying to clear your name, Doctor Stockmann! And if you refuse to cooperate, if that's going to be your attitude . . .

DR. STOCKMANN: Yes? Go on. What will you do?

HOVSTAD, *to Aslaksen:* I think we'd better go.

DR. STOCKMANN, *stepping in their way:* What will you do? I would like you to tell me. Me, the man two minutes ago you were going to make into a hero—what will you do now that I won't pay you?

ASLAKSEN: Doctor, the public is almost hysterical . . .

DR. STOCKMANN: To my face, tell me what you are going to do!

HOVSTAD: The Mayor will prosecute you for conspiracy to destroy a corporation, and without a paper behind you, you will end up in prison.

DR. STOCKMANN: And you'll support him, won't you? I want it from your mouth, Hovstad. This little victory you will not deny me. *Hovstad starts for the door. Dr. Stockmann steps into his way.* Tell the hero, Hovstad. You're going to go on crucifying the hero, are you not? Say it to me! You will not leave here until I get this from your mouth!

HOVSTAD, *looking directly at Dr. Stockmann:* You are a madman. You are insane with egotism. And don't excuse it with humanitarian slogans, because a man who'll drag his family through a lifetime of disgrace is a demon in his heart! *He advances on Dr. Stockmann.* You hear me? A demon who cares more for the purity of a public bath than the lives of his wife and children. Doctor Stockmann, you deserve everything you're going to get!

Dr. Stockmann is struck by Hovstad's ferocious conviction. Aslaksen comes toward him, taking the budget out of his pocket.

ASLAKSEN, *nervously:* Doctor, please consider it. It won't take much money, and in two months' time I promise you your whole life will change and . . .

Offstage Mrs. Stockmann is heard calling in a frightened voice, "What happened? My God, what's the matter?" She runs to the front door. Dr. Stockmann, alarmed, goes quickly to the hallway. Ejlif and Morten enter. Morten's head is bruised. Petra and Captain Horster enter from the left.

MRS. STOCKMANN: Something happened! Look at him!

MORTEN: I'm all right, they just . . .

DR. STOCKMANN, *looking at the bruise:* What happened here?

MORTEN: Nothing, Papa, I swear . . .

DR. STOCKMANN, *to Ejlif:* What happened? Why aren't you in school?

EJLIF: The teacher said we better stay home the rest of the week.

DR. STOCKMANN: The boys hit him?

EJLIF: They started calling you names, so he got sore and began to fight with one kid, and all of a sudden the whole bunch of them . . .

MRS. STOCKMANN, *to Morten:* Why did you answer!

MORTEN, *indignantly:* They called him a traitor! My father is no traitor!

EJLIF: But you didn't have to answer!

MRS. STOCKMANN: You should've known they'd all jump on you! They could have killed you!

MORTEN: I don't care!

DR. STOCKMANN, *to quiet him—and his own heart:* Morten . . .

MORTEN, *pulling away from his father:* I'll kill them! I'll take a rock and the next time I see one of them I'll kill him!

Dr. Stockmann reaches for Morten, who, thinking his father will chastise him, starts to run. Dr. Stockmann catches him and grips him by the arm.

MORTEN: Let me go! Let me . . . !

DR. STOCKMANN: Morten . . . Morten . . .

MORTEN, *crying in his father's arms:* They called you traitor, an enemy . . . *He sobs.*

DR. STOCKMANN: Sssh. That's all. Wash your face.

Mrs. Stockmann takes Morten. Dr. Stockmann stands erect, faces Aslaksen and Hovstad.

DR. STOCKMANN: Good day, gentlemen.

HOVSTAD: Let us know what you decide and we'll—

DR. STOCKMANN: I've decided. I am an enemy of the people.

MRS. STOCKMANN: Tom, what are you . . . ?

DR. STOCKMANN: To such people, who teach their own children to think with their fists—to them I'm an enemy! And my boy ... my boys ... my family ... I think you can count us all enemies.

ASLAKSEN: Doctor, you could have everything you want!

DR. STOCKMANN: Except the truth. I could have everything but that—that the water is poisoned!

HOVSTAD: But you'll be in charge.

DR. STOCKMANN: But the children are poisoned, the people are poisoned! If the only way I can be a friend of the people is to take charge of that corruption, then I am an enemy! The water is poisoned, poisoned, poisoned! That's the beginning of it and that's the end of it! Now get out of here!

HOVSTAD: You know where you're going to end?

DR. STOCKMANN: I said get out of here! *He grabs Aslaksen's umbrella out of his hand.*

MRS. STOCKMANN: What are you doing?

Aslaksen and Hovstad back toward the door as Dr. Stockmann starts to swing.

ASLAKSEN: You're a fanatic, you're out of your mind!

Mrs. Stockmann, grabbing Dr. Stockmann to take the umbrella: What are you doing?

DR. STOCKMANN: They want me to buy the paper, the public, the pollution of the springs, buy the whole pollution of this town! They'll make a hero out of me for that! *Furiously, to Aslaksen and Hovstad:* But I'm not a hero, I'm the enemy—and now you're first going to find out what kind of enemy I am! I will sharpen my pen like a dagger—you, all you friends of the people, are going to bleed before I'm done! Go, tell them to sign the petitions! Warn them not to call me when they're sick! Beat up my children! And never let her—*he points to Petra*—in the school again or she'll destroy the immaculate purity of the vacuum there! See to all the barricades —the truth is coming! Ring the bells, sound the alarm! The truth, the truth is out, and soon it will be prowling like a lion in the streets!

HOVSTAD: Doctor, you're out of your mind.

He and Aslaksen turn to go. They are in the doorway.

EJLIF, *rushing at them:* Don't you say that to him!

DR. STOCKMANN, *as Mrs. Stockmann cries out, rushes them with the umbrella:* Out of here!

They rush out. Dr. Stockmann throws the umbrella after them, then slams the door. Silence. He has his back pressed against the door, facing his family.

DR. STOCKMANN: I've had all the ambassadors of hell today, but there'll be no more. Now, now listen, Catherine! Children, listen. Now we're besieged. They'll call for blood now, they'll whip the people like oxen— *A rock comes through a remaining pane. The boys start for the window.* Stay away from there!

MRS. STOCKMANN: The Captain knows where we can get a ship.

DR. STOCKMANN: No ships.

PETRA: We're staying?

MRS. STOCKMANN: But they can't go back to school! I won't let them out of the house!

DR. STOCKMANN: We're staying.

PETRA: Good!

DR. STOCKMANN: We must be careful now. We must live through this. Boys, no more school. I'm going to teach you, and Petra will. Do you know any kids, street louts, hookey-players—

EJLIF: Oh, sure, we—

DR. STOCKMANN: We'll want about twelve of them to start. But I want them good and ignorant, absolutely uncivilized. Can we use your house, Captain?

HORSTER: Sure, I'm never there.

DR. STOCKMANN: Fine. We'll begin, Petra, and we'll turn out not taxpayers and newspaper subscribers, but free and independent people, hungry for the truth. Oh, I forgot! Petra, run to Grandpa and tell him—tell him as follows: NO!

MRS. STOCKMANN, *puzzled:* What do you mean?

DR. STOCKMANN, *going over to Mrs. Stockmann:* It means, my dear, that we are all alone. And there'll be a long night before it's day—

A rock comes through a paneless window. Horster goes to the window. A crowd is heard approaching.

HORSTER: Half the town is out!

MRS. STOCKMANN: What's going to happen? Tom! What's going to happen?

DR. STOCKMANN, *holding his hands up to quiet her, and with a trembling mixture of trepidation and courageous insistence:* I don't know. But remember now, everybody. You are fighting for the truth, and that's why you're alone. And that makes you strong. We're the strongest people in the world . . .

The crowd is heard angrily calling outside. Another rock comes through a window.

DR. STOCKMANN: . . . and the strong must learn to be lonely!

The crowd noise gets louder. He walks upstage toward the windows as a wind rises and the curtains start to billow out toward him.

The Curtain Falls.

FOR THE BEST IN PAPERBACKS, LOOK FOR THE

In every corner of the world, on every subject under the sun, Penguin represents quality and variety—the very best in publishing today.

For complete information about books available from Penguin—including Penguin Classics, Penguin Compass, and Puffins—and how to order them, write to us at the appropriate address below. Please note that for copyright reasons the selection of books varies from country to country.

In the United States: Please write to *Penguin Group (USA), P.O. Box 12289 Dept. B, Newark, New Jersey 07101-5289* or call 1-800-788-6262.

In the United Kingdom: Please write to *Dept. EP, Penguin Books Ltd, Bath Road, Harmondsworth, West Drayton, Middlesex UB7 0DA.*

In Canada: Please write to *Penguin Books Canada Ltd, 90 Eglinton Avenue East, Suite 700, Toronto, Ontario M4P 2Y3.*

In Australia: Please write to *Penguin Books Australia Ltd, P.O. Box 257, Ringwood, Victoria 3134.*

In New Zealand: Please write to *Penguin Books (NZ) Ltd, Private Bag 102902, North Shore Mail Centre, Auckland 10.*

In India: Please write to *Penguin Books India Pvt Ltd, 11 Panchsheel Shopping Centre, Panchsheel Park, New Delhi 110 017.*

In the Netherlands: Please write to *Penguin Books Netherlands bv, Postbus 3507, NL-1001 AH Amsterdam.*

In Germany: Please write to *Penguin Books Deutschland GmbH, Metzlerstrasse 26, 60594 Frankfurt am Main.*

In Spain: Please write to *Penguin Books S. A., Bravo Murillo 19, 1° B, 28015 Madrid.*

In Italy: Please write to *Penguin Italia s.r.l., Via Benedetto Croce 2, 20094 Corsico, Milano.*

In France: Please write to *Penguin France, Le Carré Wilson, 62 rue Benjamin Baillaud, 31500 Toulouse.*

In Japan: Please write to *Penguin Books Japan Ltd, Kaneko Building, 2-3-25 Koraku, Bunkyo-Ku, Tokyo 112.*

In South Africa: Please write to *Penguin Books South Africa (Pty) Ltd, Private Bag X14, Parkview, 2122 Johannesburg.*